The Puerto Ricans

Consulting Editors

THE IMMIGRANT EXPERIENCE

The
Puerto Ricans

Jerome J. Aliotta

Sandra Stotsky, General Editor
Harvard University Graduate School of Education

CHELSEA HOUSE PUBLISHERS

New York • Philadelphia

CHELSEA HOUSE PUBLISHERS

Editorial Director: Richard Rennert
Executive Managing Editor: Karyn Gullen Browne
Copy Chief: Robin James
Picture Editor: Adrian G. Allen
Creative Director: Robert Mitchell
Art Director: Joan Ferrigno
Production Manager: Sallye Scott

THE IMMIGRANT EXPERIENCE

Editors: Rebecca Stefoff and Reed Ueda

Staff for THE PUERTO RICANS

Assistant Editor: Annie McDonnell
Copy Editor: Apple Kover
Assistant Designer: Stephen Schildbach
Cover Illustrator: Jane Sterrett

First Printing

1   3   5   7   9   8   6   4   2

Library of Congress Cataloging-in-Publication Data

Aliotta, Jerome J.
   The Puerto Ricans / Jerome J. Aliotta.—[2nd ed.]
   p. cm.—(The immigrant experience)
   Includes bibliographical references (p.) and index.
   ISBN 0-7910-3360-0.
       0-7910-3382-1 (pbk.)
   1. Puerto Ricans—United States—Juvenile literature. 2. Puerto Rico—Juvenile literature.
I. Title. II. Series.
E184.P85A55   1995   95-10125
305.868′7295073—dc20   CIP
                                                                     AC

CONTENTS

Introduction: "A Nation of Nations"   7

The Citizen Immigrants   13

The Island and Its People   19

In Search of Prosperity   39

Life on the Mainland   43

Picture Essay: A Cultural Celebration   49

A Complex Heritage   71

Prominent Puerto Ricans   81

The Future Generation   101

Further Reading   104

Index   107

THE IMMIGRANT EXPERIENCE

A LAND OF IMMIGRANTS

THE AFRICAN AMERICANS

THE AMERICAN INDIANS

THE AMISH

THE ARAB AMERICANS

THE CHINESE AMERICANS

THE CUBAN AMERICANS

THE GERMAN AMERICANS

THE GREEK AMERICANS

THE HAITIAN AMERICANS

ILLEGAL ALIENS

THE IRISH AMERICANS

THE ITALIAN AMERICANS

THE JAPANESE AMERICANS

THE JEWISH AMERICANS

THE KOREAN AMERICANS

THE LEBANESE CHRISTIANS

THE MEXICAN AMERICANS

THE POLISH AMERICANS

THE PUERTO RICANS

THE RUSSIAN AMERICANS

Other titles in preparation

CHELSEA HOUSE PUBLISHERS

A
NATION OF
NATIONS

Daniel Patrick Moynihan

The Constitution of the United States begins: "We the People of the United States. . ." Yet, as we know, the United States was not then and is not now made up of a single group of people. It is made up of many peoples. Immigrants and bondsmen from Europe, Asia, Africa, and Central and South America came here or were brought here, and still they come. They forged one nation and made it their own. More than 100 years ago, Walt Whitman expressed this great central fact of America: "Here is not merely a nation, but a teeming Nation of nations."

Although the ingenuity and acts of courage of these immigrants, our ancestors, shaped the North American way of life, we sometimes take their contributions for granted. This fine series, *The Peoples of North America*, examines the experiences and contributions of different immigrant groups and how these contributions determined the future of the United States and Canada.

Immigrants did not abandon their ethnic traditions when they reached the shores of North America. Each ethnic group had its own customs and traditions, and each brought different experiences, accomplishments, skills, values, styles of dress, and tastes in food that lingered long after its arrival. Yet this profusion of differences created a singularity, or bond, among the immigrants.

The United States and Canada are unusual in this respect. Whereas religious and ethnic differences have sparked intolerance throughout the rest of the world—from the 17th-century religious wars to the 19th-century nationalist movements in Europe to the near extermination of the Jewish people under Nazi Germany— North Americans have struggled to learn how to respect each other's differences and live in harmony.

Our two countries are hardly the only two in which different groups must learn to live together. There is no nation of significant size anywhere in the world which would not be classified as multi-ethnic. But only in North America are there so *many* different groups, most of them living cheek by jowl with one another.

This is not easy. Look around the world. And it has not always been easy for us. Witness the exclusion of Chinese immigrants, and for practical purposes Japanese also, in the late 19th century. But by the late 20th century, Chinese and Japanese Americans were the most successful of all the groups recorded by the census. We have had prejudice aplenty, but it has been resisted and recurrently overcome.

The remarkable ability of Americans to live together as one people was seriously threatened by the issue of slavery. Thousands of settlers from the British Isles had arrived in the colonies as indentured servants, agreeing to work for a specified number of years on farms or as apprentices in return for passage to America and room and board. When the first Africans arrived in the then-British colonies during the 17th century, some colonists thought that they too should be treated as indentured servants. Eventually, the question of whether the Africans should be treated as indentured, like the English, or as slaves who could be owned for life was considered in a Maryland court. The court's calamitous decree held that blacks were slaves bound to a lifelong servitude, and so also were their children. America went through a time of moral examination and civil war before it finally freed African slaves and their descendants. The principle that all people are created equal had faced its greatest challenge and survived.

Yet the court ruling that set blacks apart from other races fanned flames of discrimination that burned long after slavery was abolished—and that still flicker today. Indeed, it was about the time of the American Civil War that European theories of evolution were turned to the service of ranking different peoples by their presumed distance from our apelike ancestors.

When the Irish flooded American cities to escape the famine in Ireland, the cartoonists caricatured the typical "Paddy" (a common term for Irish immigrants) as an apelike creature with jutting jaw and sloping forehead.

By the 20th century, racism and ethnic prejudice had given rise to virulent theories of a Northern European master race. When Adolf Hitler came to power in Germany in 1933, he popularized the notion of an Aryan race. Only a man of the deepest ignorance and evil could have done this. *Aryan* is a Sanskrit word, which is to say the ancient script of what we now think of as India. It means "noble" and was adopted by linguists—notably by a fine German scholar, Max Müller—to denote the Indo-European family of languages. Müller was horrified that anyone could think of it in terms of race, especially a race of blond-haired, blue-eyed Teutons. But the Nazis embraced the notion of a master race. Anyone with darker and heavier features was considered inferior. Buttressed by these theories, the German Nazi state from 1933 to 1945 set out to destroy European Jews, along with Poles, Gypsies, Russians, and other groups considered inferior. It nearly succeeded. Millions of these people were murdered.

The tragedies brought on by ethnic and racial intolerance throughout the world demonstrate the importance of North America's efforts to create a society free of prejudice and inequality.

A relatively recent example of the New World's desire to resolve ethnic friction nonviolently is the solution that the Canadians found to a conflict between two ethnic groups. A long-standing dispute as to whether Canadian culture was properly English or French resurfaced in the mid-1960s, dividing the peoples of the French-speaking Province of Quebec from those of the English-speaking provinces. Relations grew tense, then bitter, then violent. The Royal Commission on Bilingualism and Biculturalism was established to study the growing crisis and to propose measures to ease the tensions. As a result of the commission's recommendations, all official documents and statements from the national government's capital at Ottawa are now issued in both French and English, and bilingual education is encouraged.

The year 1980 marked a coming of age for the United States's ethnic heritage. For the first time, the U.S. Bureau of the Census asked people about their ethnic background. Americans chose from more than 100 groups, including French Basque, Spanish Basque, French Canadian, African-American, Peruvian, Armenian, Chinese, and Japanese. The ethnic group with the largest response was English (49.6 million). More than 100 million Americans claimed ancestors from the British Isles, which includes England, Ireland, Wales, and Scotland. There were almost as many Germans (49.2 million) as English. The Irish-American population (40.2 million) was third, but the next-largest ethnic group, the African-Americans, was a distant fourth (21 million). There was a sizable group of French ancestry (13 million) as well as of Italian (12 million). Poles, Dutch, Swedes, Norwegians, and Russians followed. These groups, and other smaller ones, represent the wondrous profusion of ethnic influences in North America.

Canada too has learned more about the diversity of its population. Studies conducted during the French/English conflict showed that Canadians were descended from Ukrainians, Germans, Italians, Chinese, Japanese, native Indians, and Inuit, among others. Canada found it had no ethnic majority, although nearly half of its immigrant population had come from the British Isles. Canada, like the United States, is a land of immigrants for whom mutual tolerance is a matter of reason as well as principle. But note how difficult this can be in practice, even for persons of manifest goodwill.

The people of North America are the descendants of one of the greatest migrations in history. And that migration is not over.

Koreans, Vietnamese, Nicaraguans, Cubans, and many others are heading for the shores of North America in large numbers. This mix of cultures shapes every aspect of our lives. To understand ourselves, we must know something about our diverse ethnic ancestry. Nothing so defines the North American nations as the motto on the Great Seal of the United States: *E Pluribus Unum*—Out of Many, One.

In August 1989, more than 50,000 supporters of Puerto Rican independence gathered in front of San Juan's capitol during congressional hearings on the island's future. As citizens of a U.S. commonwealth, Puerto Ricans are citizens of the United States and encounter no legal barriers in immigrating to the U.S. mainland. However, Puerto Rican immigration would be significantly affected if the island becomes an independent nation.

THE
CITIZEN
IMMIGRANTS

The Puerto Rican migration to North America is unique, for although Puerto Ricans come from a land with a different language and culture, they have been citizens of the United States since 1917. The Puerto Ricans are also the first people to have come to the U.S. mainland in a mass airborne migration. The Puerto Rican migration began in the late 19th and early 20th centuries, when a small number of Puerto Rican political refugees came to New York City. In the years after World War I (1914–18), Puerto Rican workers came to work in mainland industries. A number of them worked in and around the Brooklyn Navy Yard and settled in the New York City area. After World War II (1939–45), Puerto Ricans began coming to the United States in larger numbers. Again, although they came to many parts of the country, the majority of them came to New York.

Starting in 1945, thousands of Puerto Ricans fled the island's struggling economy, taking advantage of inex-

13

pensive flights to U.S. cities—chiefly New York City—where the postwar economy was booming. By 1950, the U.S. Bureau of the Census counted 226,110 people of Puerto Rican origin residing in the United States, a number that more than tripled the 1940 census figures of 69,967. This mass migration of Puerto Ricans lasted for several years, peaking during the 1950s, then decreasing steadily until 1976, when it began to increase again. Because there are no restrictions on travel between the island of Puerto Rico and the mainland United States, Puerto Rican migration remains high, particularly during times of U.S. economic prosperity. Some Puerto Ricans come to visit family and friends, some come as tourists, and some come on business, but the majority come in search of a good job and a new home for their families.

In 1989, the Bureau of the Census estimated that 2,330,000 people of Puerto Rican origin or descent lived in the United States. This figure represented nearly two-fifths of the worldwide Puerto Rican population; the other 3.5 million lived in the Commonwealth of Puerto Rico. Almost one-half of those Puerto Ricans in the United States resided in New York City, which boasts a Puerto Rican population second only in size to that of San Juan—Puerto Rico's capital and largest city.

As early as 1930, New York's East Harlem had come to be known as El Barrio (the Neighborhood) because of its large Puerto Rican community. Also known as Spanish Harlem, this neighborhood today remains heavily concentrated with Puerto Ricans. Along East 116th Street, El Barrio's main street, and in La Marqueta (the Market) on Park Avenue, the many small, family-run businesses—bodegas (grocery stores), cafés, and restaurants—give this area a distinct Puerto Rican flavor. In fact, these Puerto Rican enterprises dot the street of almost every Puerto Rican neighborhood in the city.

One significant effect of the Puerto Rican migration has been the growth of bilingualism in the New York

City area. The Spanish-speaking Puerto Ricans, along with other Hispanic groups such as the Cubans, have influenced the use of Spanish in public notices and signs. Wherever there are advertisements in English— on billboards, in subway cars, and on buses—there are almost certainly also advertisements in Spanish.

More than a dozen Spanish-language newspapers are available in New York City. The most popular newspaper, *El Diario-La Prensa*, is staffed mainly by Puerto Ricans. Spanish-speaking radio stations play Latin American music, particularly *salsa*—short for *salsa picante* (hot sauce)—a musical genre that combines lilting Spanish melodies, fiery African rhythms, and moody American jazz.

Spanish television has been on the air for almost two decades. In the metropolitan area, broadcast channels 41 (WXTV from New Jersey) and 47 (WNJU from New York) carry Spanish-language live variety shows, *novelas* (soap operas), Spanish and Mexican films, commercials, educational programs, and news shows.

The schools, too, have felt the Puerto Rican influence. Some schools in Puerto Rican neighborhoods have been given Spanish names; for example, Brooklyn's Public School 84 has been named José de Diego School in honor of a 19th-century Puerto Rican statesman and poet. Several hundred thousand Puerto Rican students are enrolled in the New York City public-school system. Because about one-fifth of them cannot speak English well, early childhood classes in Spanish have been added to the schools' teaching program.

The Puerto Rican population in the United States is one of the youngest of all ethnic groups. Approximately 45 percent of its members are under 20 years of age, a configuration that presents serious economic difficulties for the group. Because the Puerto Rican adult working population is generally younger and less experienced than the adult working population of other ethnic groups, individual incomes are low. For ex-

A Puerto Rican family poses in their home in South Framingham, Massachusetts. Second-generation Puerto Ricans tend to assimilate more easily into mainland society than did their parents, who faced significant linguistic and cultural barriers.

ample, in 1980 the median Puerto Rican family income in New York City was $8,705—30 percent below the city's average.

Several factors have inhibited the Puerto Ricans' advancement out of poverty. One of these factors is the relative youth and inexperience of the Puerto Rican population in the United States. Many Puerto Ricans come to the mainland without the education or training required for obtaining skilled jobs. Nevertheless, as with most immigrant groups, the second-generation Puerto Ricans in New York (known as "Neoricans" or "Nuyoricans") have gained entrance into professional and technical jobs faster than their parents. They have also experienced greater success in bringing the social and political concerns of the Puerto Ricans to the attention of U.S. citizens and lawmakers.

The town of Barranquitas lies in the northeast foothills of the Cordillera Central. Although tourists usually associate Puerto Rico with the narrow strip of low-lying land along its tropical beaches, steep-sloped mountains dominate three-fourths of the island's terrain.

THE ISLAND AND ITS PEOPLE

Puerto Rico, an island 111 miles long and 36 miles wide, lies in the Caribbean Sea about 1,000 miles southeast of Miami, Florida, and 540 miles north of Venezuela. It is one among a dense cluster of 7,000 tropical islands—the largest of which is Cuba—that form the West Indies. Puerto Rico belongs to a particular group of islands called the Greater Antilles. Puerto Rico has been associated with the United States since 1898, when Spain ceded the island colony as part of a peace agreement following the Spanish-American War.

The island of Puerto Rico is the uppermost portion of an enormous mountain submerged in the depths of the Caribbean. Three-fourths of Puerto Rico's terrain is mountainous or hilly, offering a variety of scenic landscapes and geological formations. Though Puerto Rico is located in an area called the tropical zone, its considerable distance from the equator and the steady trade winds from the northeast help keep temperatures at a comfortable average of 82 degrees in the summer and in the mid-70s in the winter. The southern and western areas of the island are warmer, as the Cordillera Central mountain range blocks the trade winds from the north. While a completely sunless day in Puerto Rico is something of a rarity, rain does fall steadily throughout the year (averaging a heavy 75 inches annually), varying in extent from the highlands to the lowlands and falling more heavily from May to December. Puerto Rico's climate is ideal for agriculture, yet only one-third of the soil is considered of good quality, and much of the soil along the northern coast has been covered over by housing development.

The island's landscape is very rich in vegetation, and three-fourths of Puerto Rico was once covered with trees. Many of them were cut down for fuel and housing. Today, less than one-fourth of the island is tree covered. The felling of trees over the years has added to the problems of flooding and erosion and has also contributed to the modern-day problem of global warming and ozone depletion. While factories and industry pollute the environment and coastal waters with their refuse, much of Puerto Rico's countryside remains untainted by modernization.

Puerto Rico boasts more than 200 species of birds. Many birds from North America migrate there in the winter or to the islands farther south. In the bright blue waters off Puerto Rico's northern and western coasts are beautiful coral reefs with their colorful marine life. The curious observer can watch (either through a glass-bottom boat or from underwater with a swimming mask) various sea horses, sea porcupines, starfish, crabs, and a brilliant array of tropical fish swimming in Puerto Rico's coastal waters.

In 1952, the island became a U.S. commonwealth (*estado libre asociado* in Spanish) when Congress passed a bill permitting the Puerto Rican government to write and amend its own constitution as long as its provisions did not conflict with the U.S. Constitution. As commonwealth citizens of the United States, Puerto Ricans are subject to most federal laws but are virtually independent politically. They cannot vote in U.S. presidential elections but may vote in presidential primaries. Puerto Rico elects a resident commissioner to the U.S. House of Representatives. The commissioner cannot vote on bills on the floor of the House but may vote in committees to which he or she is assigned.

One of the chief benefits of commonwealth status is that Puerto Ricans pay no taxes to the federal government. From time to time movements within Puerto Rico seek to make the island either completely independent or the 51st state of the United States, but many Puerto Ricans see drawbacks to both of these positions. If Puerto Rico became completely independent, the island would lose the substantial aid it receives from the United States and would have to support itself by its own taxes; if it became a state, its citizens would have to begin paying federal taxes. In a referendum in December 1993, Puerto Ricans rejected statehood and voted to continue the commonwealth status.

With the backing of dollars from the mainland, Puerto Rico has transformed its traditional agrarian economy into one chiefly devoted to manufacturing, led by pharmaceutical companies, businesses that produce electrical equipment, and manufacturers of food products. Tourism, which brings more than 1.5 million visitors to the island annually, is another important source of income. As a commonwealth, Puerto Rico is able to attract U.S. companies by offering significant and wide-ranging tax exemptions on profits and on interest earned from deposits made in local banks. Business incentives of this nature have helped Puerto Rico attain a per capita income estimated to be the highest in Latin America.

Still, Puerto Rico's 1988 per capita income of $5,157 was considerably lower than that of Mississippi, the poorest U.S. state, and its unemployment rate is almost three times that of any state. Economic disparities such as these help explain why a vast number of Puerto

Juan Ponce de León, the first Spanish governor of Puerto Rico, led the earliest wave of Spanish colonists to the island. For more than three centuries, Spain used Puerto Rico primarily as a military outpost to defend the trade routes of its empire, linking Mexico, the Caribbean, and South America to mainland Spain.

Ricans have moved to the U.S. mainland since World War II. The continual migration of people to and from the mainland United States leaves an ever greater imprint of U.S. culture and economy upon the island. Yet, despite the increasing influence of the United States, centuries of control by Spain have left a distinctive Spanish influence on Puerto Rico's culture and life-style.

Spanish Domination: The First 300 Years

On November 19, 1493, while sailing through the Caribbean Sea, Christopher Columbus came upon a large tropical island called Borinquén by its 30,000 Taino Indian inhabitants. Columbus renamed the island San Juan Bautista (St. John the Baptist) in honor of Don Juan, the son of his Spanish patrons, King Ferdinand and Queen Isabella. Columbus triumphantly returned to Spain with samples of gold, plants, fruits, colorful birds, and several Taino. Almost immediately, Columbus was sent back to the island to establish another Spanish colony in the New World. He returned with a large fleet of ships bearing 1,200 Spaniards from all walks of life. Among these men was Juan Ponce de León, a soldier who had distinguished himself in Spain's war against the Moors of Granada. Ponce de León's arrival would have dire consequences for the Taino.

Somewhat shorter than the Europeans of the day, the Taino had reddish tan skin; straight, long black hair; and high cheekbones. As people who fished and lived in small, peaceful tribes along the island's shore, they were unprepared for the Spanish conquistadores who invaded their island. The Taino had only primitive weapons—bows and arrows, axes, and a type of wooden sword called the *macana*—and they were easily overpowered by the well-armed Spaniards.

In August 1509, King Ferdinand appointed Ponce de León the first governor of the island of San Juan and ordered him to distribute both the land and the conquered Taino Indians to the colonists. Ponce de León sent to Spain for his wife and his children and built a large house in Caparra, the first Spanish settlement. In November 1511, the Caparra settlement, located on the northern coast near present-day San Juan, was renamed Puerto Rico (Rich Port). King Ferdinand honored the island by granting it its own coat of arms, which is one of the oldest ones in use today in the Western Hemisphere.

By 1521, the city of Puerto Rico had been moved across the bay, and its name was changed to San Juan. Eventually it became the capital city, and the island took on the name of Puerto Rico. In the meantime, the island's gold supplies were discovered to be less plen-

Workers haul sugarcane from fields near Guánica in 1942. Sugarcane has been Puerto Rico's most important crop since the 16th century. Today, however, most of the farming and processing of the cane is mechanized.

tiful than had originally been thought, and agriculture was proposed as the means to support the colony. Beginning in 1518, black slaves, whom plantation owners considered stronger and more skillful than the Taino, were imported from Africa to work the land and tend the livestock. Before long, about one-third of the Taino and many Spaniards died in a smallpox epidemic that apparently had been carried to the island by the African slaves. By 1530, the Taino population was practically nonexistent—its members had been either killed by the Spaniards, fallen victim to disease, or forced off the island.

Puerto Rico's history of racial intermixture and intermarriage dates from the 16th century. When the Spanish colonized the island, the Taino population began to die out. Beginning in 1518, slaves were imported from Africa to replace the Taino as laborers (slavery remained a part of Puerto Rican society until it was abolished by King Amadeo of Spain in 1873). Because few Spanish women accompanied the colonizers to the Americas, Spanish men in Puerto Rico interbred with and married Taino and African women. During the late 18th century, in an effort to stimulate the island's economy, Spain encouraged new settlers and entrepreneurs to migrate to Puerto Rico. As a result, people of several ethnic backgrounds began to populate the island: Dominicans, Haitians, Venezuelans, Canary Islanders, and French people from Louisiana who fled their homes when the United States purchased the territory in 1803.

These migrations produced a rich ethnic and racial blend. The skin color of Puerto Ricans today ranges from fair to black, and the islanders use a number of terms to describe gradations of color and racial characteristics. The term *de color* is most commonly used in reference to a dark-skinned or black person. The word most commonly used for people with light brown skin is *trigueno*, which describes the majority of the Puerto Rican population. *Indio* is used for a person with Indian features, while *grifo* denotes a light-skinned person with kinky hair. *Blanco*, a term equivalent to "white" in the United States, refers to light-skinned people. The names *negro/negra* and *negrito/negrita* are terms of endearment for anyone of any color, including white. In Puerto Rico, prejudice or discrimination is usually directed at class distinctions rather than at skin color. The *barrio* (district or neighborhood) in which people live is an indication of their class standing, as is their level of education. Those in the middle or upper classes are often white or light skinned, while those in the lower classes are often people of color.

Puerto Rico's agricultural economy was based on the cultivation of sugarcane. The island's warm weather was ideal for growing the crop, and slaves provided a cheap source of labor. Several sugar mills were set up, and experts in sugarcane processing were brought in from the Canary Islands, a Spanish colony located off the western coast of Morocco. By 1570, income from the sugar industry had spawned an economic boom, but this period of prosperity soon came to an abrupt end. It became increasingly expensive to obtain slaves for the sugarcane plantations, and many trading ships were attacked by pirates on the largely unpoliced waters surrounding the island. Then came war.

With its rival England intent on conquering new lands, Spain decided to build up its military forces in San Juan. The city became the key defense post for Spain's closely ruled colonies in the Americas, most of which were located along the Gulf of Mexico and the Atlantic coast. In 1595, the English privateer Sir Francis Drake attacked and captured San Juan. But his soldiers, unaccustomed to fighting battles in the blazing sun and pouring rain, suffered severely, and Spain regained control of the island. The Dutch followed with an attack in 1622 and burned a sizable portion of the city. In response to these invasions, the Spanish transformed San Juan into a walled city guarded by three fortresses, La Fortaleza, El Morro, and San Cristóbal.

By the mid-17th century, the sugar industry had sharply declined, and landowners began instead to raise cattle and grow ginger and tobacco. In an effort to monopolize Puerto Rico's trade, the Spanish government restricted Puerto Rico to trading only with Spain. As shipping traffic to the island gradually slackened over the years (during one seven-year period not a single ship from Europe entered San Juan's harbor), the colonists, unable to buy and sell goods legally, were forced to develop a black market commerce with neighboring British, French, and Dutch islands. Puerto Rico's economy thrived on smuggling for several decades while the island's officials ignored the illicit trade and lined their own pockets with a portion of the profits. At the same time, the population began to swell as foreigners, fleeing revolutions in other lands, sought refuge in Puerto Rico. In 1690, there had been only 6 towns along the northern coast; by 1750, there were 14.

In 1765, the Spanish government decided to clamp down on Puerto Rico's smuggling industry, to encourage commerce, and to improve agricultural practices. It sent a distinguished Irish soldier named Alexander O'Reilly to investigate Puerto Rico's economic and military condition. O'Reilly made several recommendations: that the sugar processing industry be revived, that farmers from Spain be sent to help cultivate the land, that Spain relax its trade restrictions and allow Puerto Rico to trade with other nations, and that the military services and defense of the island be reinforced. As a result of O'Reilly's recommendations, Puerto Rico developed a thriving legal commerce and a fortified military presence.

In 1797, after Spain and France declared war on Great Britain, 60 British frigates bearing 7,000 troops laid siege to San Juan. After a monthlong series of skirmishes, Puerto Rican forces halted the British advances. In gratitude for its valiant defense against the invading British, Spain's King Charles IV granted Puerto Rico a 20-year tax exemption on commerce and ordered promotions within its military.

Uphill to Independence

As the 19th century began, the vast majority of Puerto Ricans demanded more autonomy from Spain, reforms in education, reductions in taxes, the right to form labor unions, and the right of Puerto Rican natives to be appointed to government positions. Ramón Power, a liberal reformist, traveled to Spain as a representative of

At the outset of the Spanish-American War in 1898, the United States ousted Spain from Puerto Rico. U.S. troops, such as this 5th cavalry squadron entering the town of San Germán, were welcomed by many Puerto Ricans who hoped to benefit from the transfer of power.

the Puerto Rican people in Spain's Cortes (Parliament). In March 1812, the Cortes adopted a more liberal constitution. Though few of Power's demands were met, the new Spanish constitution declared that Puerto Ricans were no longer colonial subjects but citizens of Spain.

Within the following 12 years, the 1812 constitution was revoked, restored, and then revoked again, so that by 1823, Puerto Rico was a colony once again. That same year, on behalf of the citizens of Puerto Rico, their deputy, José María Quiñones, presented a bill to Spain again requesting that the island natives, rather than the unsympathetic Spanish officials, direct their own lives. Spain's response came in 1825. Instead of granting independence to Puerto Rico, Spain further tightened its reins on the island. For the next 42 years, Puerto Rico was ruled by 14 different Spanish military governors.

El Grito de Lares

On the night of September 23, 1868, thereafter known as El Grito de Lares (the Cry of Lares), liberal patriots, bearing firearms, knives, and machetes, marched into the small western city of Lares and declared independence for Puerto Rico. They took the town easily and arrested the mayor and conservative leaders. But a day later, the revolt was crushed by government troops. Many of the rebels fled to the mountains and engaged in small guerrilla skirmishes with the government forces. In the process, hundreds of people who had not taken part in the insurrection were jailed. El Grito de Lares had failed. Nevertheless, the uprising became a symbol of Puerto Rico's fight for independence. In 1969, Puerto Rican governor Luis A. Ferré declared September 24 an official holiday.

Throughout the late 19th century, revolutionaries campaigned vigorously for a Puerto Rican republic; for their efforts, many of them suffered atrocities at the hands of the military. In 1897, Spain's new liberal prime minister, Práxedes Mateo Sagasta, signed the Autonomous Charter, an agreement that gave Puerto Rico the right of self-rule. However, Spain still appointed the governor, who retained the authority to dissolve the legislature and to suspend the rights of Puerto Rico's citizens. This ambiguous status of restricted autonomy proved to be short-lived.

The U.S. Invasion

In April 1898, the Spanish-American War broke out. Fighting began in Cuba and the Philippines, and on July 25, 1898, General Nelson A. Miles landed in the south-western Puerto Rican town of Guánica with 16,000 U.S. troops. They overpowered the Spanish forces after less than three weeks of fighting, and Spain surrendered what remained of its control over Puerto Rico.

The Puerto Ricans gave little resistance to the U.S. invasion; they were overjoyed to see 405 years of Spanish domination come to an end. They knew that the United States was a wealthy country founded on democratic principles, and they hoped that the spirit of democracy might extend to their island in the form of a liberal and progressive government.

At the same time, a Puerto Rican independence leader named Eugenio María de Hostos was organizing the League of Patriots in New York City. The League demanded the transition from a military government to a civil government and argued that the citizens of Puerto Rico should themselves decide between annexation and independence in a plebiscite (a direct vote by the people to choose their own form of government). But when the United States met with Spain in postwar negotiations, the Puerto Rican officials who were present had no say in determining the fate of the island. Under the provisions of the Treaty of Paris, signed in April 1899, Spain ceded Puerto Rico and the Philippines to the United States, and Cuba became a U.S. protectorate.

In the early years of U.S. rule, the language barrier compelled U.S. and Puerto Rican leaders to use translators in discussing political and economic issues, a situation that caused tension on both sides and a good deal of resentment on the part of the Puerto Ricans. Cultural differences, including the language barrier and Puerto Rico's extremely poor economy, forced the United States to give serious debate to the island's future. The Foraker Act, in effect from 1900 to 1916, made Puerto Rico a U.S. territory in which the residents were neither American citizens nor citizens of an independent nation. The U.S. military government, which

had maintained order during the transitional period, was replaced by a civil administration that included Puerto Ricans elected to the House of Delegates. The U.S. president appointed a U.S. governor to head the House of Delegates. Though intended to grant a measure of freedom to the Puerto Ricans, the Foraker Act incited the outrage of island leaders who had hoped for a larger degree of independence from a na-

President Harry S. Truman signs a bill in 1947 that changes the governorship of Puerto Rico to an elected office in the following year. In the interim, the U.S. Congress appointed the first native Puerto Rican governor, Jesús T. Piñero (second from right).

In 1949, Luis Muñoz Marín (with gavel) became the first native governor elected by the Puerto Rican people. The Muñoz administration initiated Operation Bootstrap, an economic program aimed at improving the island's standard of living.

tion that had promised to bring liberal policies to a country long dominated by the absolute rule of Spain.

During the second decade of the century, a significant number of Puerto Ricans expressed a desire to become U.S. citizens. On March 2, 1917, President Woodrow Wilson signed the Jones Act, which granted U.S. citizenship to all Puerto Ricans except the few who refused it. The Jones Act also made the new Puerto Rican citizens subject to the U.S. military draft, although they were not required to pay U.S. federal taxes. The act did not change the government of the island; a U.S.-appointed governor continued to appoint executive and judicial officials and to veto legislation.

The change to U.S. rule brought a surge of economic growth to Puerto Rico. The island's products, particularly sugar, found an eager market in the United States. By 1939, the acreage of Puerto Rico's cane plantations had increased sevenfold. Corporations built new roads and mills to boost sugar production. Sugar had always been important to Puerto Rico's economy; by 1940, however, it dominated the island. More than three-fourths of all Puerto Ricans were directly or indirectly dependent upon the sugar industry.

There were negative aspects to this economic boom. Many family farms were absorbed by the sugar plantations and turned over to cane, and as a result, the island could no longer feed itself and had to begin importing

In 1954, police seize three Puerto Rican nationalists after they opened fire in the House of Representatives, wounding five congressmen. When Rafael Cancel Miranda (center) and his companions, Lolita Lebrón (left) and Andrés Cordero (right), were released from prison in 1979, crowds of independentistas jammed the streets of San Juan to cheer Miranda, who had become a symbol of their dream of nationhood.

food. Economic growth tended to benefit the land-owners and corporations more than the average Puerto Rican worker. At the same time, Puerto Rico experienced a sudden population explosion as U.S. administrators introduced new public-health measures—such as clean drinking water and better medical care—that kept more Puerto Ricans alive longer than ever before. The pressures of a fast-growing population contributed to the economic stress felt by the middle- and lower-class islanders. When the demand for Puerto Rican sugar began to wane in the 1940s, the island began to shift from a mostly agricultural economy to one in which manufacturing and industry played a significant part, but the loss of agricultural jobs, together with the rising population, created a high rate of unemployment.

American rule also brought changes to the island's educational system. Compulsory education—in which all children are required by law to attend school—was introduced in 1899. It took decades, however, for the reality of education in Puerto Rico to catch up to the law. By the 1960s, more than 95 percent of all school-age children were attending classes. Teaching is in Spanish in Puerto Rico's public schools; English is taught as a second language.

During the 1920s and 1930s, demands to upgrade the condition of the island persisted, but the U.S. Congress was slow to act. Theodore Roosevelt, Jr., served as governor of Puerto Rico (1929–32), and he encouraged various economic, educational, and cultural programs and favored more personal liberty for the Puerto Ricans. However, in the late 1930s, violence broke out in Ponce when the police interfered with a Nationalist party parade. Nineteen people were killed and nearly 100 people were wounded. In response to this violent episode, two bills demanding independence for the island were introduced in the U.S. Congress, but neither bill passed, apparently because members of Congress believed that the island's economic and social circumstances had to be improved before Puerto Rico's political situation could be determined.

The Commonwealth

In 1946, the United States appointed the first native Puerto Rican, Jesús T. Piñero, to the post of governor. One year later, Congress passed the Elective Governors Act, granting the Puerto Ricans the right to elect their own governor and empowering the governor to appoint all officials except the auditor and members of the Supreme Court. The first native governor elected by the people of Puerto Rico was Luis Muñoz Marín, who took office in January 1949. The Muñoz administration played a leading role in supporting Operation Bootstrap, a joint Puerto Rican and American project aimed at making the island self-sufficient and at raising its standard of living by building an industrial economy.

During Muñoz's years in office, Puerto Rico also acquired the new political status of commonwealth, which gave the island further autonomy, its own flag, and, with the 1950 enactment of the Puerto Rican Federal Relations Act, the opportunity to write its own constitution, as long as its provisions did not overstep the limitations placed on a territory of the United States. Congress approved the constitution of the commonwealth, which came into effect on July 25, 1952, the 54th anniversary of the landing of U.S. troops at Guánica. This date, called Constitution Day, is Puerto Rico's most important civil holiday. It is celebrated with both parades and demonstrations, indicating the Puerto Ricans' complex feelings about their commonwealth status.

In the past four decades, the question of civil status has fueled much heated discussion among the islanders. A small minority, led by the Independence party, demands complete independence or nationhood; another minority, represented by the New Progressive party (formerly the Party for Statehood), would like to see Puerto Rico become the 51st state; the majority of the people, represented by members of the Popular Democratic party (begun by Muñoz in 1938), have called for the continuation of Puerto Rico's current status as a commonwealth.

Some have sought to achieve their political goals through terrorist acts, particularly those people in favor of nationhood. In 1950, two New York–based Puerto Rican nationalists traveled to Washington and attempted to assassinate President Harry S. Truman; Muñoz was also one of their targets. On March 1, 1954, three Puerto Ricans, led by 25-year-old Rafael Cancel Miranda, fired shots from the gallery of the U.S. House of Representatives, wounding several congressmen. Today, the most renowned of Puerto Rican terrorists, Los Macheteros, continue to fight for independence. In 1983, to finance its operations the group robbed an armored car company in West Hartford, Connecticut, of $7.1 million.

During the 1980s, the mood in Puerto Rico seemed to indicate a growing desire for a change in status. In June 1989, 80,000 Puerto Ricans participated in a rally for independence. Puerto Rico's political status was hotly debated in both the United States and Puerto Rico. President George Bush was quoted as saying that he favored statehood for the island; on the other hand, Puerto Rico's governor Rafael Hernández Colón said in 1990, "I am firmly convinced that statehood is not in the best interest of Puerto Rico or the United States. I believe that the present commonwealth relationship should be continued and enhanced." The governor rejected the "inflexibility of statehood," seeing the commonwealth status as "a noble experiment in flexible political relationships for people with different cultures," a reasonable status for an island whose culture reflects aspects of both North and South America. A third point of view is held by another, smaller group within Puerto Rico, the *independentistas*. They would like to see Puerto Rico become a fully independent nation.

When Puerto Ricans went to the polls in 1993 to vote on the issue of statehood versus commonwealth status, they rejected statehood. The majority of Puerto Ricans agree that commonwealth status is the best way to maintain their identity as a people with their own language, culture, and traditions while at the same time continuing to receive the benefits of a close association with the economically and militarily powerful United States. These supporters of commonwealth status argue that statehood would bring financial ruin to the island by taking away its exemption from federal income taxes and destroying its status as a tax haven. They also point out that nationhood, the route favored by the independentistas, would also have financial drawbacks: Puerto Rico would lose the social welfare programs and business incentives that its relationship with the United States now provides.

Although most Puerto Ricans now come to the mainland by air, this family disembarked in New York City from a boat in 1947 after selling their home to pay for their passage. More than 2.3 million Puerto Ricans now live on the U.S. mainland.

IN SEARCH OF PROSPERITY

One of the most significant factors contributing to the first wave of Puerto Rican migration to the United States was a population explosion on the island. It had taken more than 400 years after Columbus's discovery of Puerto Rico for the population to grow to 1 million people. But in the first 25 years of the 20th century, because of improved medical services and public health systems instituted when Puerto Rico became a U.S. territory, the island's population doubled to 2 million. The small and once sparsely inhabited island quickly became one of the most densely populated regions in the Western Hemisphere. In 1990, an estimated 3.5 million *puertorriqueños* lived on the island.

During the first quarter of the 20th century, despite some gains in economic development, Puerto Rico's standard of living remained far below that of the United

Two mothers attend their children in a San Juan slum in 1941. Even though economic programs, such as Operation Bootstrap, have improved housing, services, roads, and factories over the past 50 years, unemployment in Puerto Rico has remained high. Many Puerto Ricans migrate to the mainland in search of greater economic opportunity for themselves and their children.

States's, and its unemployment rate soared far above. Large U.S. corporations owned a large portion of the prospering sugarcane plantations, thereby cornering much of the island's wealth. During these early years, migration to the mainland was very small; a boat trip to the United States cost more than the average Puerto Rican earned in a year. In 1910, only 1,513 Puerto Ricans lived in the continental United States. However, in subsequent decades, deteriorating economic and social conditions and a series of natural disasters—including the hurricanes of 1928 and 1932—prompted thousands of Puerto Ricans to consider emigration as their only means of survival. By 1930, 52,774 Puerto Ricans were living on the mainland.

In the years before the Great Depression of the 1930s, the sugarcane industry provided one-sixth of Puerto Rico's total income and two-thirds of its export dollars: It also generated approximately one-fourth of the jobs on the island. One out of every three factories in Puerto Rico was related to the sugarcane industry—including sugar mills, rum distilleries, and molasses plants. When sugar prices on the world market fell during the depression, the island's economy was seriously threatened.

In 1935, a federal law that set 25 cents as the nation-wide minimum hourly wage severely crippled the needlework industry, which at the time employed about 40,000 women. Employers had been paying only about one-sixth that amount. As a result of the enactment of the law, those employers who could not afford the wage hike abandoned the industry, putting thousands of women out of work. Over the next five years, the amount earned by needlework exports fell by nearly three-fourths. The minimum wage also nearly wiped out revenues in the tobacco industry. Puerto Rico was torn apart by unemployment, mass starvation, and growing political unrest.

Puerto Rico's economic crisis continued during World War II when German submarines in the Caribbean Sea halted the shipping of food and supplies. Because the German military presence also made travel to the mainland extremely hazardous, migration was generally low. But that was soon to change.

LIFE
ON THE MAINLAND

In the late 19th century, the first Puerto Ricans to come to the United States were political exiles engaged in a battle for independence from the powerful Spanish military regime. One of the more prominent exiles was Ramón Emeterio Betances, whose reformist ideas—which included the demands for the abolition of slavery and for freedom of speech—angered the governor of Puerto Rico. Emeterio fled first to Santo Domingo, the capital of the Dominican Republic, and then to New York City, where he and other abolitionists formed the first movement aimed at the formation of an independent Puerto Rican republic.

In 1891, the journalist Francisco Gonzalo "Pachin" Marín moved to New York City, where he published a revolutionary newspaper, *El Postillón*, that had been suppressed by the Puerto Rican government. In 1898, another reformer, Eugenio María de Hostos, organized the League of Patriots in New York City to fight for

Puerto Rico's transition from a military regime to a civil government. Luis Muñoz Rivera joined other Puerto Ricans in New York City to help fight for an independent government in Puerto Rico, full civil rights for its people, and free commerce with the United States. In 1948, his son, Luis Muñoz Marín, would become Puerto Rico's first elected governor.

Santiago Iglesias Pantín, considered the father of Puerto Rico's labor movement, also spent time in New York City. Iglesias was a Spanish-born socialist who arrived in Puerto Rico in 1896 after being deported from Cuba, where for nine years he had fought for workers' rights. In Puerto Rico, he formed the Socialist party, a branch of the American Socialist party, and he worked to gain prolabor legislation. Iglesias also founded the union called the Federación Libre de Trabajadores (FLT), whose members were chiefly low-paid, seasonal sugarcane cutters. The FLT, which was affiliated with the American Federation of Labor, survived for 40 years. Iglesias's Socialist party made some important gains for workers during its peak years, between 1915 and 1924. Puerto Rico's Labor Day, celebrated on the first Monday in September, is called Santiago Iglesias Day in Iglesias's honor.

Starting in the City

The Puerto Ricans who came to New York City during World War I established their first major settlement around the Brooklyn Navy Yard. Before long, they also began to settle in the area of Manhattan called Harlem, which was becoming increasingly populated by blacks as well. In 1920, approximately 7,300 Puerto Ricans were living in New York City, and the prosperous years of the Roaring Twenties enticed many more to move to the mainland. By 1930, nearly 53,000 Puerto Ricans had migrated—more than a 300 percent increase in only 20 years. However, throughout the 1930s and early 1940s, migration slowed down because of scarce economic opportunities during the Great Depression and the global turmoil of World War II.

After the war, however, the Puerto Rican population in New York City began to expand into East Harlem and across the Harlem River into the South Bronx. In subsequent years, Puerto Rican communities spread outward from these neighborhoods into the Williamsburg section of Brooklyn, as well as into Manhattan's West Harlem, its Lower East Side, Upper West Side, and "Hell's Kitchen" (an area west of 8th Avenue and between 42nd and 57th Streets). The popular and highly acclaimed musical *West Side Story* depicts the racial tension resulting from this population expansion in Hell's Kitchen. It tells the story of a gang of teenage boys fighting Puerto Rican youths, whose growing numbers were encroaching upon their turf.

Puerto Rican migration peaked during the 1950s, and by 1960 nearly 900,000 Puerto Ricans were reported to be living on the mainland. Since then, although migration has decreased, it still remains significant. Today, New York City's Puerto Rican population has expanded into all five boroughs, with the smallest Puerto Rican population on Staten Island and the next smallest in Queens.

Migrant Farm Workers

Not all Puerto Ricans migrated directly to urban areas in the United States. In the 1930s, U.S. employers turned to Puerto Rico for farm laborers. By 1940, Puerto Ricans had become a significant part of the stream of migrant workers who flowed along the Atlantic coast. A large percentage of farm laborers in Puerto Rico were employed in the harvesting of sugarcane, seasonal work that begins in January and ends in June or July. Because harvesting seasons on the mainland coincided with inactive periods in Puerto Rico, year-round employ-

Migrant laborers from Puerto Rico harvest a crop on a New Jersey farm. Once the sugarcane harvest is completed in Puerto Rico in June, many Puerto Rican farm workers travel to the mainland to help U.S. farmers bring in their crops.

ment was possible for a large number of Puerto Rican workers who were willing to travel between the island and the mainland.

Conditions for workers in unregulated migrant pools were extremely harsh; long hours, inadequate housing, and extremely low wages were the norm. Puerto Rican migrants faced the additional hardship of not speaking English. In the mid-1940s, newspapers in both Puerto Rico and the United States ran stories on the injustices of the migrant labor system. In 1947, two laws were passed requiring mainland farm employers who hired native Puerto Ricans to provide contracts approved by Puerto Rico's Department of Labor. Farm labor contracts guaranteed a Puerto Rican worker a set number of hours for a given month with a clearly stated wage. The contracts also made provisions for housing, food, medical care, insurance, and transportation to and from the island. The Office of the Commonwealth of Puerto Rico, established on the mainland in 1948, was responsible for monitoring employers to ensure that the conditions of these contracts were carried out.

Since these laws were passed, an average of 20,000 contract farm workers have come to the mainland each year. They harvest potatoes on Long Island, fruits and vegetables in New Jersey, tobacco in Connecticut, and sugar beets in Michigan. Employers are required to pay for their workers' return flight to Puerto Rico as long as they have fulfilled the conditions of their contracts.

The farm labor contracts by no means solved all the difficulties faced by Puerto Rican migrant workers. Nevertheless, many workers were exposed to life on the mainland. In addition to being employed, they were able to familiarize themselves with the cities or towns near the farms where they worked, to explore the possibility of permanent employment, and to establish a base if conditions for permanent migration seemed promising. However, when Puerto Ricans did seek to establish themselves permanently in small cities and towns near farm areas, they often became the target of discrimination. Cultural, linguistic, and racial barriers in the United States were only slowly diminishing.

Puerto Ricans living on farms and in rural areas of the United States represent a very small percentage of the population who immigrate to the mainland; about 95 percent of Puerto Rican immigrants settle in urban areas. By far, the greatest number of Puerto Ricans have settled in New York City and its surrounding communities. In 1970, there were more Puerto Ricans living in New York than in San Juan, though by 1980 these numbers had reversed. The concentration of Puerto Ricans in New York City cannot be explained by geographic proximity; there are many large U.S. cities closer to Puerto Rico. It is likely that the general pattern of Puerto Rican migration was established during the pre–World War II years, when boat travel to New York, the nation's leading port city, was the norm. The postwar immigrants, who most often traveled by plane, tended to join relatives already established in New York City's Puerto Rican community.

The Great Migration

The significant influx of Puerto Ricans into the United States, known as the great migration, began at the close of World War II and lasted until the mid-1960s. By the end of the war in 1945, thousands of unemployed and underpaid Puerto Ricans were ready to migrate to the mainland, where jobs were plentiful. Unlike other immigrant groups, Puerto Ricans, as U.S. citizens, encountered no legal or political restrictions preventing them from moving to the United States. Moreover, transportation to the mainland had become relatively inexpensive and fast; a person could travel from San Juan to New York City in an average of 6 hours for $50 or less. Travel agencies in Puerto Rico provided credit arrangements for those people who could not afford the price of a ticket.

Because Puerto Rican migration is to a large extent economically motivated, many Puerto Ricans living on the U.S. mainland perceive themselves as being in economic exile. Those who came during the post–World War II years did not increase their income by as great a percentage as had some earlier immigrants; nevertheless, their wages almost always doubled. The average weekly income of Puerto Ricans who came to New York City just after World War II was $28.05 for their first job, as compared to $14.60 for their last job in Puerto Rico.

Studies of Puerto Rican migration to the United States have shown that a majority of the migrants are unemployed in Puerto Rico and come to the United States seeking jobs. In 1986, for example, 69 percent of all Puerto Ricans who migrated to the mainland were unemployed. The figure was even higher for women.

(continued on page 57)

A CULTURAL CELEBRATION

Overleaf: *Waving a* pava *(the straw hat traditionally worn by rural Puerto Ricans) and the flag of their homeland, Puerto Ricans celebrate their heritage during the annual Puerto Rican Day parade in New York City. Nearly half of the 2.3 million Puerto Ricans living on the U.S. mainland reside in New York City.* Below: *Members of a Puerto Rican softball team show their enthusiasm before a game in New York City's Central Park.* Right: *Puerto Rican musicians provide a steady beat for the people hanging out in Central Park.*

Left: *The Puerto Rican Traveling Theater performs a play during a street festival in Harlem, a section of New York City where many Puerto Ricans live.* Above: *Puerto Rican actors perform in a New York City production of* Winterset, *a play written by Puerto Rican Miriam Colón.*

Puerto Rican dancers wearing traditional costumes march during a parade celebrating the Fiesta del Apóstol Santiago.

A Puerto Rican children's choir sings during the Fiesta de los Tres Reyes Magos (Festival of Three Kings) celebration held in a New York City church. The youthful Puerto Rican community faces many challenges as it attempts to assimilate into mainstream U.S. society without losing touch with its cultural heritage.

(continued from page 48)

Many Puerto Rican women with children to support turned to the aid provided by U.S. welfare policies. As many as a third of all households in some Puerto Rican communities are headed by women, and only one-quarter of these female heads of households are in the labor force; the others depend largely upon public assistance. The public-housing projects of the New York City area, despite their bleakness and their chronic crime problems, offer a form of security to these women.

Frequent travel between the island and the United States—an enduring pattern that began in the early days of the Puerto Rican migration—has made it difficult to determine how many Puerto Ricans are coming to the mainland for the first time. It is also uncertain how many are planning to make the United States their permanent residence or how many of those returning to the island will remain there permanently. Census figures are calculated by determining the difference between the number of persons arriving from Puerto Rico and the number of those departing. But these net figures are deceptive because they greatly understate the massive movement of people. For example, in 1955, 343,720 Puerto Ricans arrived on the mainland and 298,256 departed—both figures are much higher than the 45,464 net migration. In certain years—1961 and 1963, for example—more Puerto Ricans left the United States than entered, resulting in a negative migration, though more than 1 million people moved between the island and the mainland in each of these years.

In general, the migration of Puerto Ricans to the mainland has been influenced by economic trends. When the availability of jobs in the United States is high, the number of immigrants increases. A reverse migration usually occurs during periods of labor saturation and economic recession in the United States and during periods of improving employment conditions on the island. Many social scientists also believe that return

Young Puerto Rican mothers gather on a New York City street. Female-headed households are numerous in the Puerto Rican community. For example, in 1980 nearly 44 percent of Puerto Rican families in New York City were headed by females, compared to the citywide average of 26 percent.

migration is due in part to the inability of some Puerto Ricans to adjust to the very different culture of the mainland. The deep love of the homeland and its proximity to the United States provide other strong incentives for Puerto Ricans to return to the island. If discouraged by the new culture, unemployment, or the language barrier, Puerto Ricans can board a plane and be back home in a matter of a few hours.

Family Life

Puerto Ricans have traditionally emphasized the importance of family as a primary source of strength and support, especially during the process of migration. Puerto Rican families are generally large. Among the Puerto Rican immigrants who came to the mainland in the late 1940s, one-third were from families with 10 or more members and about two-thirds were from families with 6 or more. Even today, Puerto Ricans have the largest families of all New York City residents.

The Puerto Rican family structure follows no single pattern. Extended family households, which include relatives other than the parents and children, are as common as nuclear families. It is not uncommon for a Puerto Rican household to include a father and a mother, their children, and children of a former marriage or another union. Female-headed households are numerous; the 1980 U.S. census reported that almost 44 percent of all Puerto Rican families in New York City were solely female headed, compared to approximately 26 percent in the entire city.

A consensual union—or a bond between a man and a woman without benefit of a civil or religious marriage ceremony—was once a common phenomenon, particularly among poor islanders; but in recent years the practice has fallen out of favor. Many factors have contributed to this recent decline, particularly among those Puerto Ricans who have moved to the mainland. Proof of marriage is required in order to obtain certain valuable economic benefits, such as a widow's pension, Social Security, and, in New York City, admittance to public housing. Because consensual unions have long been associated with the poor, people of the lower classes who aspire to rise to the middle class tend to choose a legal union. In addition, the influence of education and the Roman Catholic church, as well as the shifting role of women, have contributed to the decline of consensual unions.

A traditional feature of the Puerto Rican family is the superior authority exercised by the man, an authority based upon a stubbornly held belief that men are inherently superior to women. The behavior that is a result of this attitude is known as *machismo*, or maleness. The man assumes the role of head of the household and makes the decisions for all of its members, without asking for his wife's or family members' consent.

Machismo allows men more social freedom than that accorded women and is often associated with sexual prowess and power. In Puerto Rico, it is customary for women to be virtually dominated by men. In Puerto Rican communities in the United States, however, women benefit from greater opportunities of employment and education, resulting in a decline in the prevalence of machismo. Moreover, if a woman can gain independence in no other way than by leaving her husband, greater economic opportunity and public welfare on the mainland assure the survival of her family.

Life in New York City

Although there are some clearly identifiable Puerto Rican neighborhoods, Puerto Ricans have tended to spread out. They are now found in virtually every part of New York City. This is because much of the housing within the income of many of the migrants is public housing, which is regulated by the New York City Housing Authority and is scattered throughout the city. Such housing is assigned to applicants on a nondiscriminatory basis, so the buildings are inhabited by people of all races and all cultures.

In 1980, slightly more than 50 percent of Puerto Rican families living on the mainland had annual incomes of less than $10,000, and the income of nearly half of those families was under $5,000. By comparison, the median family income for all Americans in 1980 was approximately $20,000. Nevertheless, Puerto Rican families living on the mainland are economically better off than families living on the island, where the median income in 1980 was less than $6,000.

One reason for the generally low income level among Puerto Ricans is their relatively young age. In 1980, the average age of Puerto Ricans in New York was 22 years—much younger than the average age of the American population as a whole. The Puerto Rican migrants are young, overall, because the population of

Puerto Rico itself is relatively young; Puerto Rico is still experiencing the population boom that began in the 1930s. Some of the economic and social disadvantages that Puerto Ricans face in the United States are related to their youth. For example, age greatly affects income, especially in professions that require experience and education, and younger people are likely to earn less money than older workers. The Puerto Rican population is also confronted with the same problems that affect other young people in America—teenage pregnancy and illegitimacy, poor attendance in school, and lack of male role models in female-headed households—but such problems are especially severe among a population that contains so high a percentage of teenagers and young adults.

Since the postwar years, the majority of Puerto Ricans on the mainland have held blue-collar jobs—jobs that require less training and education than white-col-

A Puerto Rican worker sews in a garment factory in Queens, New York. Many Puerto Rican women work in the city's garment industry.

lar jobs. Thus, many Puerto Ricans are employed in the hotel and restaurant businesses as bellhops, dishwashers, and buspersons and in hospitals as orderlies. Puerto Rican women make up a large segment of the garment industry, an industry that traditionally has employed the city's most recent immigrants (currently Asian immigrants, especially Chinese women, are also heavily represented in the garment industry).

A good education and a command of the English language are linked to the ability to get a good job. Second-generation Puerto Ricans have made employment advances that can be attributed, for the most part, to their generally higher level of education. For men, the advancement is usually into the categories of craftsmen, foremen, and skilled workers. Both men and women now perform white-collar clerical and sales work. Recent decades have seen a significant increase in the number of primarily second-generation Puerto Ricans, both men and women, in professional and technical jobs. In 1980, about 14 percent of all Puerto Ricans in the United States were in professional or technical fields, compared with only about 8 percent in 1950. Despite this improvement, however, the Puerto Ricans lag behind American society as a whole, possibly because they continue to lag behind in education as well. In 1980, about 22 percent of Puerto Ricans in New York City were high-school graduates, compared with 30 percent of whites and 33 percent of blacks.

Many of the educational difficulties experienced by Puerto Ricans on the mainland can be attributed to the language barrier. For the last three decades, Puerto Rican students in New York City public schools have accounted for about one-fourth of the student population. During these decades the city school system has been challenged as never before by budgetary constraints and increased responsibilities. Wealthy New Yorkers have tended to send their children to private schools, and many observers believe that the quality of public education in the city has declined dramatically. For Puerto Ricans who may have been raised in a Spanish-speaking household, this decline in educational standards has been particularly harmful because, until recently, few Puerto Rican students had received any special help for their language handicap. The New York City Board of Education was slow to respond to the needs of Puerto Rican students, largely because of the shortage of bilingual teachers and the lack of funds for bilingual programs.

Since 1970, however, New York City has added a number of Spanish-speaking teachers and bilingual programs to its school system. Supporters of bilingual education argue that such programs give the children of immigrants a better chance to receive a good education. Yet the effectiveness of bilingual education has not been proved beyond question, and critics of bilingualism feel that it actually hurts Spanish-speaking children by eliminating their motivation to learn English, which remains the key to full participation in the American workplace and in society in general. The best bilingual programs teach children English while offering Spanish-language instruction in the standard curriculum for those whose English is not yet good enough for English-language classes.

A Puerto Rican educational association called Aspira (Aspire) has played a major part in campaigning nationwide for bilingual teaching in schools with substantial numbers of Puerto Rican students. It has been instrumental in developing and promoting programs to improve general educational conditions and opportunities for Puerto Ricans. Aspira also devotes time to helping Puerto Rican youths build self-confidence and develop a sense of identity within the larger community. It also helps to find scholarships and financial aid for promising Puerto Rican students who want to attend college.

In January 1970, members of the Young Lords party, a Puerto Rican student activist group, file out of court after being arrested for occupying a New York City church. The efforts of the Young Lords, which included various protests and demonstrations, brought recognition to the educational needs of the city's young Puerto Ricans.

In 1970, recognition of the difficulties faced by blacks and Puerto Ricans who wanted to attend college but were financially or educationally lacking prompted the City University of New York to adopt an "open admissions" policy. In 1980, many more Puerto Ricans had finished college than in 1970, although the percentage of Puerto Rican graduates was still far below the national average. The educational level for Puerto Ricans 25 years old and older remains 2 years behind the national average. These statistics have not escaped conscientious educators, among them Puerto Ricans who believe that the first step toward better education of students is better education of the public.

In the 1960s, large numbers of Puerto Rican students participated in aggressive demonstrations and protests in the colleges and universities, protests that brought widespread recognition to the needs of young Puerto Ricans. Led by an activist group called the Young Lords party, students caused the City University of New York to shut down for a time in the spring of 1969. They were also instrumental in the birth of Puerto Rican studies programs at Queens, Brooklyn, and Lehman Colleges. The Puerto Rican students ultimately played a major role in developing a sense of identity among all Puerto Ricans and those of Puerto Rican descent. Puerto Rican studies programs are now found in the curricula of most New York City colleges and many private colleges, and these same institutions also sponsor and support Puerto Rican student organizations and associations.

Several Puerto Ricans have become prominent in the academic world. Antonia Pantoja, the founder of Aspira, also established the Universidad Boricua (Puerto Rican University) in Washington, D.C., a place for talented Puerto Rican students to pursue advanced scholarship in Puerto Rican issues and concerns. Since 1972, Frank Bonilla has directed the Puerto Rican Studies Center at the City University of New York. For many years Luis Quero Chiesa was chairman of the Board of Higher Education for New York City, and from 1984 to 1987, Nathan Quiñones served as chancellor of New York City's Board of Education. Another prominent New York City educator, Joseph A. Fernandez, was born in East Harlem to Puerto Rican parents. After dropping out of high school to join the U.S. Air Force, Fernandez obtained a high-school equivalency diploma in the service. After leaving the service he attended Columbia University to study mathematics in preparation for a teaching career. He rose through the public-school administration system to serve as New York City's superintendent of schools, but he was ousted from this post in 1993 after he introduced a controversial first-grade teaching guide with a "rainbow curriculum" approach that emphasized minorities, including homosexuals; many parents' and church groups, including some Hispanic groups, felt that this subject matter was inappropriate for young children.

Although Puerto Ricans constitute a substantial part of the New York City population, only a small proportion are eligible voters because of the youthful composition of the group. Compounding this problem is the large number of Puerto Ricans who are not registered to vote. Weak participation and underrepresentation in U.S. politics is a pattern common among immigrant groups that engage in back-and-forth migration between their homeland and the United States. An interest in local and national politics seems, however, to be on the increase among Puerto Ricans living on the mainland, and by 1989 New Yorkers had elected one Puerto Rican U.S. congressman, one Puerto Rican borough president, four Puerto Rican state senators, four Puerto Rican state assemblymen, and three Puerto Rican city councilmen. The Puerto Rican community boasts several elected judges. And in 1990, thousands of Puerto Rican New Yorkers petitioned for the right to vote in the proposed 1991 statehood plebiscite in Puerto Rico.

Communities Outside of New York

As early as 1920, there were Puerto Rican communities outside of New York in such cities as Chicago, Boston, Miami, and New Orleans. Others formed in the post–World War II years of increased migration. In 1980, nearly 90 percent of the Puerto Ricans living in the United States were concentrated in the larger cities of just 8 states—New York, New Jersey, Illinois, Florida, California, Pennsylvania, Connecticut, and Massachusetts. The remaining 10 percent were dispersed relatively evenly throughout the rest of the nation.

The Puerto Rican community in Chicago, which began to grow during World War II, has consistently ranked as the second largest on the mainland. In 1980, the city was home to 112,000 Puerto Ricans. Although Chicago's Puerto Rican population is scattered around the city even more than the Puerto Rican population in New York City, Chicago's largest Puerto Rican community is located on its Northwest Side. In New York, Puerto Ricans constitute the majority of Spanish-speaking peoples, but in Chicago they are dwarfed by a much larger Mexican population. In recent years, an increasing number of Cubans and other Spanish-speaking groups have also joined the Puerto Ricans and Mexicans in Chicago.

In its early years, Chicago's Puerto Rican community established an organization called the Caballeros de San Juan (Knights of St. John) to promote leadership among Puerto Ricans and to advance and preserve their religious, political, and cultural interests within the larger community. This society was a source of support for the community in the late 1950s and early 1960s.

In the late 1950s, the Commonwealth of Puerto Rico established a second mainland office in Chicago, which has served the needs of the Puerto Rican populations in East Chicago, Milwaukee, Gary, Detroit, and other midwestern cities and has also protected the rights of contract farm laborers in the midwestern states.

The Puerto Rican communities in New Jersey—particularly Jersey City, Hoboken, Newark, and Paterson—are a spillover of the Puerto Rican population in New York. Other Puerto Rican communities in Nassau and Suffolk counties on Long Island were created by contract farm workers who decided to settle there. Bridgeport, Connecticut, has attracted many farm laborers because of its nearby tobacco farms. There is also a large Puerto Rican community in Florida, especially in Miami, but Puerto Ricans in these places are far

Business leaders of the Puerto Rican community in New York City meet with the head of the U.S. government's Small Business Administration in 1964 in the hope of forming a similar agency for Puerto Ricans in that city.

outnumbered by the Cubans, who are relatively affluent and wield more political power. Philadelphia is home to another large Puerto Rican community, ranked third behind New York City and Chicago in population size. Over the last two decades, a large number of Puerto Rican families have settled temporarily in Boston. Many of these new immigrants are transient laborers who have come to the United States to earn enough capital to return to Puerto Rico to purchase land.

Small numbers of Puerto Ricans first came to the small, highly industrialized cities of Lorain and Youngstown, Ohio, during World War II. Attracted by jobs in factories (in Lorain, a Ford Motor Company plant), machine shops, and steel mills, they found steady work, joined labor unions, and settled in neighborhoods of one- and two-family houses. Today, the majority of these people are homeowners. Puerto Ricans in these cities have developed close relationships with Spanish-speaking parishes, which have proved a vital component in preserving community identity and strength. The Puerto Ricans in Lorain, for example, have had a more active voice in both local and national elections than have less cohesive Puerto Rican communities in larger cities.

In California, Puerto Ricans have also made the transition into the mainland's foreign culture with relative ease. San Francisco and Los Angeles have fairly well established and stable Puerto Rican communities, although the number of Mexican Americans in these cities far outnumber the Puerto Rican population. The Puerto Rican communities in San Francisco and Los Angeles report the highest level of education and the smallest percentage of people living below the poverty line of all mainland Puerto Rican communities. Many Puerto Ricans in these two cities hold either professional and managerial positions, and in 1980, of all Puerto Ricans in the United States, those in San Francisco had the highest level of income.

These sugarcane workers demonstrate the variety of racial types among Puerto Ricans. Puerto Rico has a multiracial society that encompasses a white majority, people of African and Indian origin, and those of many other ethnic backgrounds.

A
COMPLEX HERITAGE

In her book entitled *Puerto Ricans: Born in the U.S.A.*, Clara E. Rodríguez, a professor of sociology at Fordham University, discusses the unique problems faced by the Puerto Ricans, a group she characterizes as unicultural, multiracial, and integrated, as they enter North American society, which she characterizes as multiethnic, biracial, and segregated. For the Puerto Rican immigrant, perhaps the most foreign aspect of American society, after language, is its rigid biracial social structure. Puerto Ricans soon realize that social acceptance is much easier for a white person and that without this advantage, social and economic advancement can be difficult. Interestingly, several studies have shown that the Puerto Ricans of intermediate color, the trigueños, who constitute the majority in Puerto Rico, experience the most serious difficulties and express the most resistance to assimilation into the New York community. Not received as whites and often mistaken for American blacks, they have desperately tried to hold on to their Spanish language and culture, which identify them as Puerto Rican.

Puerto Ricans make a clear distinction between African Americans, whom they call *morenos*, and Puerto Ricans of color. Relations between Puerto Ricans and African Americans have often been determined by the sometimes hostile struggle for a distinctive voice in the political, social, and economic arena. Members of the two groups have sometimes seen one another as competitors for the benefits of employment and aid programs, public funds, and community leadership.

These racial or cultural tensions between Puerto Ricans and blacks in the United States came to the fore during the civil rights and black power movements of the late 1960s. Puerto Ricans, a more racially integrated people, were suddenly confronted with the same problems of discrimination that blacks faced. But because their historical experiences were so different, conflict arose between Puerto Ricans and blacks over the real content and core concerns of the civil rights movement. Blacks were primarily fighting for a rebirth of the nation's soul and a rebirth of their own racial pride; Puerto Ricans were essentially fighting for the more immediate and tangible goals of economic and educational opportunities. In the end, Puerto Ricans withdrew enthusiastic participation from a movement that they did not recognize as their own.

Patterns of Assimilation

The conflict between loyalty to one's family tradition and the desire for individual economic and social success has had an effect on Puerto Ricans similar to that experienced by earlier immigrant groups. In the process of assimilation, traditions are sometimes lost. For example, the double surname common in Puerto Rico is disappearing from use in the United States. Luis Muñoz Marín, Puerto Rico's first elected governor, was named Muñoz after his father's family and Marín after his mother's. In Puerto Rico he was called "Mr.

Muñoz Marín"; if only one family name were used, he was called "Mr. Muñoz," not "Mr. Marín." To confuse the two names would have been an insult and an embarrassment. Today, however, most Puerto Ricans in the United States use only their father's name to avoid confusion in the larger community.

The weakening of Puerto Rican heritage sometimes leads to conflict between family members of the first and second generations. Children are often caught between two cultures, the Puerto Rican culture at home, where they speak Spanish and observe traditional Puerto Rican customs, and the U.S. culture that they are exposed to at school and work. The interaction of Puerto Ricans with mainland society has also led to an increasing number of marriages between second-generation Puerto Ricans and non-Hispanics.

Tension often exists between parents and their unmarried daughters, who are acculturated to American social conventions. As in many cultures, the chastity of female adolescents is traditionally protected in Puerto Rico by keeping them from social contact with males. In some parts of the island, young girls are still chaperoned when they meet with boys. For a father to bring his daughter to marriage a virgin is considered both honorable and evidence of his success as a father.

Compared with the customs of the island, dating habits in the United States are very permissive. Quite naturally, Puerto Rican teenage girls want to be like other teenagers: They want to go out on dates without a chaperon and feel free to associate with boys in their neighborhood and at school. To tradition-minded fathers, such conduct is scandalous and reflects badly on them.

Compadrazgo, or coparenthood, is an integral part of the traditional Puerto Rican family. In Puerto Rico, children often have a second set of parents who may either be their Catholic godparents (*padrinos* in Spanish), their parents' best man and maid of honor, or simply two good friends of the family. The people involved in the relationship of compadrazgo call one another *compadres*, or coparents. Compadres form both an intimate and a formal relationship with each other; to show respect for one another, compadres will often use the formal pronoun *usted* for "you," instead of the familiar *tú*. They depend on one another for economic support, for emotional encouragement, and for advice. A compadre is expected to meet all the needs of his or her fellow compadre without fail. However, this support system of compadrazgo is falling out of use among many urban Puerto Ricans today.

The Puerto Rican Family Institute, founded in the early 1960s, is a grass-roots agency that helps Puerto Rican families in New York City confront the problems of adjusting to a new way of life. The institute is staffed by Puerto Ricans, and it creates a receptive atmosphere for immigrants in a strange land. It promotes compadrazgo as a way of preventing the breakdown of the Puerto Rican family, and it tries to deter Puerto Rican youths from getting into trouble with the law. As a means of fostering a smooth transition to life in the United States, the institute attempts to match established mainland Puerto Rican families with newly arrived ones.

From the *Pueblo* to the Parish

Like most Hispanics, Puerto Ricans are predominantly Roman Catholic. But to be a Roman Catholic in Puerto Rico does not mean the same thing that it does on the mainland. On the island, Catholicism implies identification with a *pueblo* (community) and with religious values larger than the individual's. It does not necessarily mean being a believer who holds strictly to doctrine, participates regularly in the Mass, and receives the Sacraments. In the Puerto Rican tradition, the pueblo worships God in large public demonstrations, such as great fiestas, processions, and celebrations of saints' days. A Puerto Rican's worship is also likely to include a close, intimate relationship with the Virgin Mary or with several saints, who are regarded as friends and compadres. Believers hang pictures and place statuettes of these holy figures in their homes, cars, and workplaces, and they wear medals, build shrines, light candles, pray, and make vows to them. In return for such devotion, the followers hope to receive favors and protection against harm.

Although most priests in Puerto Rico in the early 20th century were Spanish rather than Puerto Rican, a significant number of priests from the United States journeyed to Puerto Rico to emphasize the character of Catholic life found on the mainland. Because few native Puerto Rican priests were available to join the members of their congregations on the mainland, Puerto Ricans who came to large cities such as New York had a difficult time retaining their traditional beliefs and practices without the support of the Puerto Rican clergy. A Puerto Rican Catholic's only choice was to join an integrated parish of the established Irish, German, and Italian groups. As the numbers of Puerto Rican worshipers grew, priests began to celebrate two masses—one in English for established residents and another in Spanish—in an effort to minister to all believers.

Over time, however, the older immigrant groups, such as the Irish and the Italians, moved on to new neighborhoods, making room for more and more Puerto Rican immigrants to take their place, until some parishes became almost completely Puerto Rican. Puerto Rican parishes soon welcomed Spanish-speaking people from Cuba, the Dominican Republic, and Central and South America as well as French- and Creole-speaking immigrants from Haiti. The Roman Catholic clergy was then faced with the problem of celebrating the Mass for people of several different languages and cultural backgrounds. The Puerto Ricans in New York have never had their own parishes around which they could build a solid community in the manner of the Germans, Irish, and Italians during the early years of the 20th century.

In 1953, the Coordinator of Spanish Catholic Action was established in the New York Archdiocese to determine the needs of newly arriving Puerto Ricans and to prompt parishes to provide special services for them. Today, many parishes and dioceses have Spanish-speaking councils. The United States Catholic Conference in Washington, D.C., has established a special staff that serves the religious and spiritual needs of Spanish-speaking people. In 1972, the mainland United States had only one Hispanic bishop. By 1990, there were 2 Hispanic archbishops and 21 Hispanic bishops; 2 of the bishops, Roberto Gonzales in Boston and Alvaro Corrada in Washington, D.C., are Puerto Rican. The Puerto Rican Catholic community hopes to see more Hispanics appointed to influential positions so that the 20 million Hispanic Catholics living in the United States today will be served more effectively.

Although Protestantism existed in Puerto Rico in the 19th century, its influence was limited and it had little lasting effect in the island's predominantly Catholic communities. When the United States annexed Puerto Rico in 1898, Protestantism received a tremendous but short-lived boost from the North American clergy who went to the island to work in schools and churches. Those Puerto Ricans who embraced Protestantism saw its emphasis on individual liberty and responsibility as an antidote to the uncompromising paternalism of the Spanish Catholic establishment.

Puerto Rican communities on the mainland support numerous Pentecostal (Christian religious congregations that seek to be filled with the presence of the Holy Ghost and that emphasize revivalistic worship, baptism, and faith healing) and evangelical sects. Members of these sects are most often the poor who have moved from the barrios to the big cities of the United States and who are acutely aware of their alienation from the traditions of their previous rural life. Small Pentecostal congregations tend to hold meetings in the storefronts of

urban neighborhoods, providing a religious experience that fills both a social and a psychological void by reinforcing the desire for proximity to the supernatural.

Despite the Catholic church's disapproval of unorthodox forms of worship, spiritualism and folk religions remain an important part of Puerto Rican spiritual life. Stores called *botánicas* sell religious paraphernalia—candles, incense, herbs, charms, and potions—that have alleged magical properties. Botánicas are found in just about every Puerto Rican neighborhood; to see several of them on a single block is commonplace. Folk practices are rooted in the belief that it is possible to contact the spiritual world of the dead. Spiritualist

Rosario, a religious ceremony purported to have curative powers, is observed by a Puerto Rican follower. A small altar is erected in a hut, and all the neighbors visit and join in prayer and the singing of hymns. Some Puerto Ricans practice various folk religions and spiritualist rituals, often in conjunction with the traditional rites of Roman Catholicism.

practices range from simple folk gatherings to séances where the spirits of the dead are believed to be conjured. Participants attempt to exert influence over spirits; they hope either to put a stop to the actions of evil spirits or to bring about the favorable deeds of good spirits.

Service Agencies

In 1948, Governor Muñoz Marín established the Office of the Commonwealth of Puerto Rico in New York City to assist the increasing number of Puerto Rican arrivals during the post–World War II migration. Over the years, the office has helped Puerto Ricans make the difficult adjustment to a large foreign city. It has helped Puerto Ricans find jobs and housing, referred them to social service resources, provided educational counseling and financial assistance to Puerto Rican students, and supervised contract programs for migrant workers.

Demonstrators walk across the Brooklyn Bridge on their way to the offices of New York City's Board of Education. The National Association for Puerto Rican Civil Rights organized the march to demand improvement in the city's educational facilities for Puerto Ricans.

The office is also a public relations center that provides information about Puerto Rico and Puerto Ricans to the larger community and information about New York and its inhabitants to Puerto Ricans.

There are many other organizations that cover a wide variety of services. The Puerto Rican Forum, a long-standing agency, represents the social, political, and business interests of Puerto Ricans nationwide. The Puerto Rican Merchants Association, one of the oldest Puerto Rican organizations in New York City, plays a major role in helping Puerto Ricans open small businesses. The Puerto Rican Teachers Association represents the needs of Puerto Rican teachers and works to increase the number of Puerto Ricans in teaching and supervisory positions. Throughout New York City, athletic leagues and cultural organizations, such as the Ateneo de Puerto Rico and the Instituto de Puerto Rico, promote cultural events, literature, and the arts. The Instituto, headed by Luis Quero Chiesa, annually honors distinguished individuals for their service to the Puerto Rican community.

Puerto Rican social clubs abound wherever large numbers of Puerto Ricans have settled. By attracting members who have migrated from the same Puerto Rican towns or villages, the clubs ease the strain of an abrupt transition to a wholly unknown way of life. Neighborhood agencies, financed by government antipoverty funds, supply an important link between neighborhood residents and the city government. They were created to provide a more open conduit between the concerns of individuals and small groups and those who are in a position to do something about these concerns.

President George Bush congratulates Dr. Antonia Novello, whom he appointed surgeon general of the United States in March 1990. Many Puerto Ricans, including Dr. Novello, have made great contributions to U.S. society.

PROMINENT PUERTO RICANS

Since the 1930s, when Puerto Ricans began moving to the mainland in significant numbers, the Puerto Rican community has made numerous and impressive contributions to the quality and character of U.S. government, business, public service, arts, music, and sports. Puerto Rican businessmen Manuel A. Casiano, Jr., and Nick Lugo both began at the bottom—the former as a delivery boy and the latter as a dishwasher—and went on to become millionaires. Herman Badillo and Robert Garcia, both Puerto Rican New Yorkers, were members of the U.S. Congress. Maurice Ferré, born in Ponce, was mayor of Miami from 1981 to 1985, and Pablo Guzman is a prominent journalist. And many talented Puerto Ricans—Tony Orlando, Geraldo Rivera, the late Freddie Prinze, and pop culture phenomenon Vanna White, to name a few—have added their unique abilities to the world of entertainment. Writers such as Jesús Colón, Piri Thomas, and Miguel Algarin have portrayed the experiences of Puerto Ricans in the United States.

Politics

Luis Muñoz Marín has dominated the Puerto Rican political arena for some time. After serving for eight years as majority leader of the Puerto Rican Senate, in 1948 Muñoz became Puerto Rico's first native to be elected governor. By the time he stepped down after his fourth term in 1964, he had been in office a total of 24 years and had become a powerful and prestigious patriarchal figure in Puerto Rico. Under Muñoz's leadership, Puerto Rico succeeded in attaining a greater amount of self-government than it had ever had before.

Muñoz was born in San Juan on February 18, 1898, 10 days after Puerto Rico won independence from Spain. His paternal grandfather had been a town mayor, and his maternal grandfather, playwright and abolitionist Ramón Marín, had been jailed by the Spanish authorities for his involvement in anticolonial campaigns. Muñoz's father, Luis Muñoz Rivera, known as the George Washington of Puerto Rico, led the independence movement that attained Puerto Rico's first measure of autonomy from Spain. Later, Muñoz Rivera became Puerto Rico's resident commissioner in the U.S. House of Representatives and has been credited with influencing Congress to grant Puerto Ricans U.S. citizenship and their own elected legislature.

Muñoz studied law at Georgetown University in Washington, D.C., and as a free-lance writer and translator, he contributed articles about Puerto Rico's colonial plight to the *Baltimore Sun*, the *New York Herald Tribune*, and several national magazines. For a short time, Muñoz lived among writers and artists in New York City and translated into Spanish the works of poets Walt Whitman, Edwin Markham, and Carl Sandburg.

Then, in 1938, Muñoz returned to Puerto Rico. Backed by a mass of young liberals, he organized the Popular Democratic party to help the islanders prepare for the economic responsibilities they would face when granted either independence or U.S. statehood. The party campaigned in the hills under the slogan *Pan, Tierra, y Libertad* (Bread, Land, and Liberty), and their emblem was the *pava*, the broad straw hat worn by the *jíbaros*, the rural peasants. Muñoz's extraordinary gift for communicating with the rural masses helped him become the most popular politician in Puerto Rican history. Today, 116th Street in East Harlem is called Luis Muñoz Marín Boulevard in his honor.

Herman Badillo, another Puerto Rican who became prominent in U.S. politics, was an 11-year-old orphan who spoke no English when he came to New York in 1940. He attended Haaren High School, supporting himself alternately as an elevator operator and as a dishwasher. In 1951, Badillo graduated magna cum laude with a degree in business administration from the City College of New York. He went on to attend Brooklyn Law School at night and in 1954 graduated cum laude. In 1965, Badillo was elected Bronx borough president, and he succeeded in bringing sizable amounts of construction funds into the Bronx. When Badillo was elected to the House of Representatives in 1970 to represent New York's 21st Congressional District, he became the first Puerto Rican member of the U.S. Congress. After serving four terms, Badillo resigned to become deputy mayor for operations under New York City mayor Edward Koch. He has served in a wide range of appointed positions in New York City government and is known for his vast knowledge of the city's complex inner workings. Badillo has always been an ardent champion of social justice and of reform for the Puerto Rican community in the United States.

In Literature

René Marqués is revered as the most important Puerto Rican playwright. In the 1950s and 1960s, Marqués used the theater as a forum for celebrating Puerto Rican pride and ethnic identity. His most famous play, *The Ox Cart*, depicts a simple farm family from the mountains of

Puerto Rico struggling to maintain the virtues of family loyalty and strength in the course of their painful adaptation to life in the United States. In the first New York City presentation of *The Ox Cart* in 1966, Puerto Rican New Yorker Raul Julia played the role of the adopted son, Luis. A recipient of a Rockefeller Foundation Fellowship, Marqués studied drama and theater arts at Columbia University. He was a professor at the University of Puerto Rico, Río Piedras, and is also the author of numerous short stories, essays, and plays.

Another Puerto Rican writer, Piri Thomas, grew up in East Harlem and attended New York City public schools. In 1950, at the age of 22, he was convicted of attempted armed robbery. He began to write in prison. The product of four years of writing was accidentally destroyed after Thomas was released from prison, and it took him another five years to rewrite *Down These Mean Streets*, his renowned autobiography, which was published in 1967. Thomas wrote the book in the dialects of Spanish Harlem and the prisons; critics admired the book's honesty and hailed the author's success in reaching audiences unfamiliar with Spanish-American slang and prison idiom. Thomas wrote a two-act play, *The Golden Streets*, which was premiered in 1970 by the Puerto Rican Traveling Theatre in New York City. He later published two more autobiographical volumes and a novel. A former drug addict, Thomas has contributed greatly for many years to drug rehabilitation programs in Spanish Harlem and Puerto Rico.

The Sports Arena

Several Puerto Rican Americans have had outstanding careers as professional athletes. Sixto Escobar (1913–79) is regarded by many as the greatest of all Puerto Rican boxers. Escobar earned a reputation as a fierce brawler, whose power-packed blows could knock an opponent senseless. At 5 feet 4 inches and 118 pounds, Escobar was in the bantamweight class; nevertheless, during sparring sessions he would often knock down lightweights, those in the 135-pound class. Escobar held the National Boxing Association's bantamweight crown 3 different times, and in 64 fights he was never knocked out. In 1939, Escobar stepped down from the throne because he could no longer make the 118-pound weight requirement. He was elected to the Boxing Hall of Fame in 1975 and died four years later in Puerto Rico.

Carlos Ortiz, a Puerto Rican–born New Yorker, won the lightweight title two times, proving himself a world-class boxer. He first won the championship at the age of 26 by defeating Joe Brown on April 21, 1962. Then, in 1965, he lost the championship, only to regain it from Ismael Laguna that same year. Born in Ponce, Puerto Rico, 5-foot-7-inch, 135-pound Ortiz began boxing professionally at the age of 19. Over the next 17 years he defended the lightweight championship 11 times. In his 70 professional fights, he was beaten only once by a knockout; the Scottish boxer Ken Buchanan delivered the blow during what turned out to be Ortiz's last fight, on September 20, 1972.

Juan A. "Chi Chi" Rodriguez, at 5 feet 7 inches and 130 pounds, has one of the most powerful swings of any professional golfer. Between the 1962 and 1963 tours, Rodriguez perfected what he calls the "solid left wall principle," a stance that has allowed him to achieve both power and distance behind his 270- to 300-yard drives. Rodriguez's book *Chi Chi's Secret of Power Golf* (1967) explains how he is able to outdistance much bigger and stronger pros. Customarily attired in a straw hat with a brightly colored ribbon, Rodriguez has long been one of golf's most popular players and crowd pleasers, known for his playful antics on the course.

One of six children, Rodriguez was born in 1935 in the Río Piedras suburb of San Juan. As a young boy, he worked as a caddie, earning 35 cents for 18 holes. In these early years, Rodriguez learned to handle clubs with power and dexterity. After serving 2 years in the

Golf legend Chi Chi Rodriguez performs his trademark sword dance after sinking a putt at the Doral Open in Miami, Florida, in 1977. Rodriguez joined the professional golf tour in 1960, and he continues to play on the senior tour for players 50 years old and over.

United States Army, he returned to Puerto Rico at the age of 21 and was hired as caddie master at the Dorado Beach Golf Club. In 1960, he joined the Professional Golfers' Association (PGA) tour. In 1963, Rodriguez won his first tournament, the Denver Open, using lightweight clubs designed for women. In 25 years on the PGA tour, Rodriguez won 8 tournaments, earning more than $1 million. In 1985, he joined the Senior Tour (for ages 50 and up) and has emerged as one of the tour's stars, winning more tournaments and earning more money in 4 years than he had in 25 years on the regular pro tour.

By far the most notable of all Puerto Rican athletes is Roberto Clemente. For his outstanding achievements as a professional baseball player and for his involvement in community activities, he has become a hero for Puerto Ricans everywhere. At the age of 17, while still in high school, Roberto received a $500 bonus to join the Santurce baseball team of the Puerto Rican League. In his third season, Clemente's sizzling .356 batting average captured the attention of major league scouts. The following year, 1955, he was signed by the Pittsburgh Pirates. In his 18 seasons with the team,

Two Puerto Rican sports greats, Carlos Ortiz (left) and Roberto Clemente (right), inspect a bat prior to a Pittsburgh Pirates game in 1966. Ortiz held the world lightweight boxing championship twice during the 1960s. Clemente, inducted into baseball's Hall of Fame in 1973, was highly acclaimed for his exceptional skills as a player and for his generous charitable contributions and service to the Puerto Rican community.

Clemente won 4 National League batting champion-ships, played in 12 All-Star games, and earned the Gold Glove Award for outstanding fielding 11 times. As an outfielder, Clemente led the league in throwing out base runners in 5 different seasons; once Clemente made a pinpoint throw from 420 feet in deep right field to nail a runner at home plate. Clemente's major league lifetime batting average was .317.

Roberto Clemente took great pride in his Puerto Rican heritage and spent much of his time off the field performing works of charity. Shortly before his death, Clemente was working on a favorite project, a "sports city" for Puerto Rican children. His career ended tragically when he was killed at the age of 38 in a plane crash off the coast of San Juan on December 31, 1972. At the time, Clemente was on a relief mission to aid earthquake victims in Nicaragua. Clemente's last base hit of the 1972 season had brought his total to exactly 3,000. He was only the 11th major league player, and the first from Latin America, to have reached this mark; to date, only 16 players have reached the 3,000-hit plateau. Roberto Clemente was inducted into the Baseball Hall of Fame in 1973; the usual five-year waiting period was waived.

Early in his career, Orlando Manuel Cepeda was called the Baby Bull to distinguish him from his famous baseball father. In 1958, Cepeda began his first major league season at the age of 21 with the San Francisco Giants and before long became one of the fans' favorite players. From 1960 to 1964, Cepeda was among the leading batters of the National League. In 1966, he was traded to the St. Louis Cardinals after a year of disability, the result of an operation on a recurring knee injury. In the same year, the Associated Press baseball writers voted Cepeda the National League Comeback Player of the Year. In 1967, Cepeda was unanimously chosen by the nation's baseball writers as the National League's Most Valuable Player.

Theater and Film

Puerto Rican–born actor-director José Ferrer was 22 years old when he made his stage debut in 1934, in a melodrama performed on a showboat in Long Island Sound. Later in his versatile career, Ferrer would be highly praised for his performances as Iago in Shakespeare's *Othello* and in the title roles of Edmond Rostand's *Cyrano de Bergerac* (stage version 1946; film version 1950) and Shakespeare's *Richard III*.

As a boy, Ferrer studied music and showed such remarkable skill at the piano that for some time it was thought he would become a concert pianist. A precocious child, he passed the entrance exams for Princeton University at the age of 14, but the school's officials determined that he was too young to enroll. When Ferrer did eventually attend Princeton, he organized a band; before long, however, he joined the Princeton Triangle Club, an acting group to which James Stewart and Joshua Logan belonged, and discovered that his real passion was the stage. Among some of his earlier stage triumphs were his parts in Maxwell Anderson's *Key Largo* (1939) and a revival of Brandon Thomas's *Charley's Aunt* (1940). In 1938, Ferrer married his first wife, German actress Uta Hagen, and together they costarred in more than a dozen productions ranging from slapstick to tragedy. In 1943, José Ferrer and Uta Hagen appeared as Iago and Desdemona in Margaret Webster's New York presentation of *Othello*, a production that went on to break the record for the longest run of a Shakespearean play in New York City history. Ferrer also appeared in many movies, including the film version of *Cyrano de Bergerac* (1950), *Lawrence of Arabia* (1962), and Woody Allen's *Midsummer Night's Sex Comedy* (1982).

Broadway song-and-dance actress Chita Rivera has been nominated for seven Tony Awards. She was awarded a Tony in 1984 for her outstanding performance as Anna in *The Rink* and again in 1993 for her starring role in *The Kiss of the Spider Woman*. Rivera was born in 1933 in Washington, D.C., as Dolores Conchita Figuero del Rivero. Her Puerto Rican father played the clarinet and saxophone with the U.S. Navy Band, sat in with the Harry James Orchestra, and played a musician in the Broadway musical *Lady Be Good*. Chita Rivera trained in classical ballet at the School of American Ballet in New York City and graduated from Taft High School in the Bronx in 1951.

Rivera began her theater career performing small roles in off-Broadway and Broadway musicals. Eventually she landed the supporting role of Anita in the landmark musical drama *West Side Story* (1957), a modern version of *Romeo and Juliet*, directed and choreographed by Jerome Robbins, with music by Leonard Bernstein and lyrics by Stephen Sondheim. The musical is about two young lovers, a Puerto Rican girl named Maria and a Polish-American boy named Tony, caught between the rivalry of two feuding street gangs. The Puerto Rican gang, the Sharks, is led by Maria's brother; Tony belongs to the "American" gang, the Jets. As Anita, Rivera sang the poignant "A Boy Like That"; the duet "I Have a Love"; and, probably the most popular song of the show, "America," a satirical song about the United States from the perspective of a Puerto Rican immigrant. The original production of *West Side Story* ran to critical acclaim for 732 performances and brought Chita Rivera her first Tony Award nomination.

On Broadway, Rivera went on to create the part of Rose in *Bye Bye Birdie* (1960); Anyanka in *Bajour* (1964); and Velma in *Chicago* (1975). In addition to her stage work, Rivera has worked in television and in film; she played the next-door neighbor Connie Richardson in the television situation comedy "The New Dick Van Dyke Show," and in 1969 she was Nickie in the movie version of *Sweet Charity*.

Puerto Rican Rita Moreno is the only performer to be the recipient of all four of the entertainment world's

most distinguished awards. In 1962, she won the Oscar for best supporting actress as Anita in the film version of *West Side Story*; in 1975, a Tony for her seething performance as Googie Gomez in Terrence McNally's Broadway comedy *The Ritz*; and in 1972, the Grammy for her participation in the sound track recording of the popular children's television series "The Electric Company." Moreno won two Emmy Awards for guest appearances on television's "The Muppet Show" in 1977 and "The Rockford Files" in 1978.

Born Rosa Dolores Alverio in Humacao, Puerto Rico, Moreno moved with her mother and several other relatives to a tenement in the Washington Heights section of Manhattan. Moreno was involved in the world of

Rita Moreno performs in a scene from the movie West Side Story. *Moreno is the only person to have received all four of the entertainment world's most distinguished awards: the Oscar, the Tony, the Grammy, and the Emmy.*

entertainment from an early age. She appeared in the children's theater in Macy's toy department, and at weddings and bar mitzvahs Moreno sometimes sported a fruit-covered headdress in impersonation of the Latin idol of the day, Carmen Miranda. After her film debut in 1950 as a delinquent in the reform-school melodrama *So Young, So Bad*, she was signed to a film contract by Metro-Goldwyn-Mayer. Her early years as a Hollywood starlet marked her as a "fiery Latin," and her controversial private life dogged her for some time. But her career took a turn for the better when director-choreographer Jerome Robbins cast her in the movie version of *West Side Story*. The film won 10 Academy Awards, including 1 for Moreno. On stage, Rita Moreno played Serafina in Tennessee Williams's *Rose Tattoo*, a performance that brought her tremendous critical acclaim. In the early 1980s, Moreno starred in the television situation comedy "Nine to Five."

Raul Julia was one of America's most distinctive and versatile stage and movie actors. Born Raul Rafael Carlos Julia y Arcelay in San Juan, Puerto Rico, Julia came to New York City in 1964 to study acting. Throughout his career, he demonstrated an ability to perform successfully in a wide range of dramatic roles in such plays as *The Castro Complex* (1970), *Where's Charley?* (1975), *The Threepenny Opera* (1976), and *Dracula* (1977). For many years he was associated with the New York Shakespeare Festival; he won considerable renown for his performances in a number of Shakespeare plays, including *Two Gentlemen of Verona* (1971) and *Hamlet* (1972). Julia reached a wide audience through his roles in a number of successful films. Among them were *The Eyes of Laura Mars*, *Kiss of the Spider Woman*, *Tequila Sunrise*, *The Addams Family*, and *Addams Family Values*. Julia devoted much of his time to the Hunger Project, an international drive to eliminate world hunger, and to the Hispanic Organization of Latin Actors (HOLA), which champions the advancement of Spanish-language theater. He died in 1994.

Puerto Rican–born Justino Díaz has established himself as one of the leading basses of the New York Metropolitan Opera. His warm basso cantante voice has been heard in a wide range of roles in Italian opera at the Metropolitan, where he debuted on October 23, 1963. Díaz has recorded performances of *Medea*, *La Wally*, and *Lucia di Lammermoor*. Born in 1940 in San Juan, Díaz studied music at the University of Puerto Rico and at the New England Conservatory and trained as an opera singer with Friedrich Jagel. Díaz has made appearances at world-renowned opera houses such as La Scala in Milan, the Hamburg State Opera, the Vienna State Opera, the Kennedy Center Opera House in Washington, D.C., and Covent Garden in London.

The World of Latin Music

Latin American music, with its roots in Caribbean islands such as Puerto Rico, Cuba, and the Dominican Republic, enjoys great popularity among music lovers in North America who crave the rousing beat of congas and timbales and the contrasting blasts of brass. From the tango in the era of silent-film idol Rudolph Valentino to the rumba, the mambo, the cha-cha, and the samba, dance crazes in North America have often coincided with revivals of Latin American music. At times, indigenous North American musical styles have influenced those of Latin America, particularly salsa. By 1930, East Harlem had developed a flourishing musical culture with clubs such as the Teatro San José on 110th Street and 5th Avenue and the Teatro Hispano on 116th Street and 5th Avenue. El Barrio had its own radio music show hosted by Julio Roque, an East Harlem dentist and musician who broadcast over WABC Radio. Roque presented local talent performing Puerto Rican *plenas*, a song form said to have originated in Ponce or

Members of Menudo, a Puerto Rican teenage singing group, hold a press conference at New York City's Hard Rock Cafe in 1987. Menudo, which means "small change" in Spanish, enjoyed worldwide popularity during the 1980s.

San Juan, and *boleros*, music designed for an accompanying Spanish dance. Later, Puerto Rican and Latin musicians were making appearances in Harlem at the Savoy Ballroom, the Apollo Theater, and the Palladium Dance Hall. These clubs featured the big bands of Tito Puente, Pablo "Tito" Rodriguez, and Machito's Afro-Cubans.

Latin Americans have brought their musical tradition to New York, Miami, Chicago, San Antonio, Philadelphia, and Los Angeles. Their audiences include not only the more than 20 million Hispanics in the United States but also the millions of people from all races who love the Latin beat. The Puerto Rican teenage singing group Menudo has had great success with North American audiences. The sultry Latin dances in *Dirty Dancing* (1987) and *Salsa* (1988) made these films big box-office hits. The movie *La Bamba* (1987), based on the life of Ritchie Valens, the first Latin to make it big in rock 'n' roll, grossed more than $50 million at the box office.

Tito Puente, percussionist, bandleader, composer, and arranger, was one of the major forces behind the fusing of Caribbean rhythms with American jazz and the bringing of the new salsa sound to the forefront of the American music scene. Known as El Rey (the King), Puente established the timbales, a pair of open-bottomed drums played from a standing position with untapered sticks, as the percussive force of the modern Latin orchestra. He is also credited with introducing the vibraphone to Afro-Cuban music. In 4 decades he has recorded more than 90 albums with his band, including the all-time best-selling salsa record entitled *Dance Mania* (1958), and at least half as many more albums with other recording artists.

The eldest son of Puerto Rican parents, Puente was born and raised in Spanish Harlem. He studied at the Juilliard School in New York City after having served three years with the U.S. Navy during World War II. Puente won recognition as an arranger and sideman before rising to stardom with his own band, the Picadilly Boys, during the late 1940s. Before long, Puente's compositions and arrangements were being played by the big Latin band leaders of the day—Machito, José Curbelo, Pupi Campo, Frank Martí, Miguelito Valdez, and Marcelino Guerra. By the early 1950s, the Tito Puente Orchestra was booking gigs in Los Angeles,

Miami, Philadelphia, and on the "Cuchifrito Circuit," the New York nightclub scene. The popularity of the mambo — a fast, staccato Afro-Caribbean dance form — was partly attributable to Puente, who preserved in his mambo more of the real rhythm of Latin music than did the big bands of the 1940s and 1950s. During the 1960s, Puente worked and recorded several albums with the celebrated Cuban vocalist Celia Cruz, who is known as La Reina (the Queen).

In 1970, Puente's career received an unexpected boost when Mexican-American rock musician Carlos

Tito Puente performs during New York City's 1990 Puerto Rican Day parade. Puente, a graduate of the distinguished Juilliard School in New York City, helped bring salsa, a musical form that combines Caribbean rhythms with jazz, to the forefront of the U.S. musical scene.

Santana recorded his interpretation of Puente's composition from the late 1950s, "Oye Como Va," which became an enormous hit. Since 1981, Puente has been occupied with his Latin Jazz Ensemble, appearing at clubs, colleges, and festivals throughout the United States and Europe, introducing Latin-style jazz to new young audiences.

The Puerto Rican–born singer-guitarist José Feliciano achieved pop recording stardom in the summer of 1968 with his Latin-soul version of the Doors' song "Light My Fire." That same year, Feliciano was awarded two Grammies, one for best male pop singer and the other for best new artist of the year. The second of eight boys, Feliciano was born blind, the victim of glaucoma, a congenital eye disease. At the age of five, Feliciano moved with his family from their farm in Lares, Puerto Rico, to New York City. They lived first at 103rd Street and Columbus Avenue and later on the Lower East Side. Virtually a self-taught musician, Feliciano has mastered the 6- and 12-string guitars, the bass, banjo, mandolin, organ, bongo drums, piano, harpsichord, harmonica, and trumpet.

In the early 1960s, when still in his teens, Feliciano began his career performing in the coffeehouses of Greenwich Village. In 1965, Feliciano recorded a solo album for RCA Victor, *The Voice and Guitar of José Feliciano*, a rhythm and blues album that included a classical Spanish guitar piece; in 1966, he made another album, *A Bag Full of Soul*. For several years Feliciano was appreciated solely by Spanish-speaking audiences, both in the United States and in Latin America. Even after the 1968 release of the album *Feliciano!*, which included his version of "Light My Fire," Feliciano was not well known outside the Hispanic community. It was not until he sang his unorthodox blues-rock rendition of "The Star-Spangled Banner" at the opening of the fifth game of the 1968 baseball World Series in Detroit that 53,000 spectators in Tiger Stadium and mil-

José Feliciano performs in Las Vegas in 1968 after his single "Light My Fire" became a hit.

lions of television viewers nationwide were finally awed by the singularity of Feliciano's talent.

Aside from the multitude of exceptionally gifted Puerto Ricans who have come to the forefront in sports, politics, music, theater, literature, and dance, millions of migrants have left a different sort of mark upon mainland society, both subtle and pervasive. Each Puerto Rican has brought a bit of the particular color of the native island with him or her—a special way of cooking, a sense of style, rituals steeped in the island's history, a particular way of practicing religion, speaking, and viewing the world. Puerto Ricans are in the unique position of being a commonwealth of the United States. They are connected to the culture of the mainland, but they also have a separate and distinct heritage. Their cultural differences cause conflicts but are also the reason Puerto Ricans have much to offer.

THE FUTURE GENERATION

Puerto Ricans have come to the United States in the hope of attaining what many other immigrant groups have been able to secure — greater opportunities in employment, education, and housing and the freedom to enjoy basic human rights and liberties. What makes them unique among other immigrant groups is that they are citizens of the United States.

Economic and social progress is difficult to measure in a population that continues to shift between its place of origin and its "second" home. Such constant movement, even if voluntary, hinders Puerto Ricans from either maintaining a strong relationship with the island and its people or from building an identity within U.S. society. Furthermore, erratic employment and schooling, the result of continual migration, contributes to the language problem that many Puerto Ricans face. Mastery of English is a prerequisite for white-collar employment. If the Puerto Rican community on the mainland is to gain greater economic security and freedom, more of its members need to possess the language skills necessary to fill positions of greater responsibility.

The future character of the Puerto Rican community in the United States depends largely on the direction taken by the second generation. In New York City, their numbers are growing; second-generation Puerto Ricans represent more than half of the Puerto Rican immigrant population, and they are on the whole still a very young group. Thus far they have achieved a remarkably higher level of education than that of their parents and are enjoying greater economic status. The rising rate of intermarriage with non–Puerto Ricans suggests

Two young Puerto Ricans read at a Bronx, New York, public library. The youthful Puerto Rican community faces many political, economic, and social challenges as it attempts to assimilate into mainstream U.S. society while at the same time preserving its cultural heritage.

that social interaction with the larger population is more acceptable than ever before. As Puerto Ricans become more intimately a part of the U.S. political and economic mainstream and as more choose to make the mainland their permanent home, Puerto Ricans are sure to win greater recognition as a distinctive and valuable part of American society, and the multiethnic culture of the United States will be enriched in the process.

FURTHER READING

Bean, Frank, and Marta Tienda. *The Hispanic Population of the United States.* New York: Russell Sage, 1987.

Chavez, Linda. *Out of the Barrio: Toward a New Politics of Hispanic Assimilation.* New York: Basic Books, 1991.

Cooper, Paulette, ed. *Growing Up Puerto Rican.* New York: Arbor House, 1972.

Cordasco, Francesco, and Eugene Bucchioni. *The Puerto Rican Experience: A Sociological Sourcebook.* Totowa, NJ: Littlefield, Adams & Co., 1973.

Fitzpatrick, Joseph P. *Puerto Rican Americans: The Meaning of Migration to the Mainland.* Englewood Cliffs, NJ: Prentice-Hall, 1971.

Garver, Susan. *Coming to America: From Mexico, Cuba, and Puerto Rico.* New York: Delacorte, 1981.

Hauberg, Clifford A. *Puerto Rico and Puerto Ricans.* New York: Twayne, 1974.

Jennings, James, and Monte Rivera, eds. *Puerto Rican Politics in Urban America.* Westport, CT: Greenwood Press, 1984.

Jiménez de Wagenheim, Olga. *Puerto Rico's Revolt for Independence.* Boulder, CO: Westview Press, 1985.

Larsen, Ronald J. *The Puerto Ricans in America.* Minneapolis: Lerner Publications, 1973.

Mapp, Edward, ed. *Puerto Rican Perspectives*. Metuchen, NJ: Scarecrow Press, 1974.

Morales Carrión, Arturo. *Puerto Rico: A Political and Cultural History*. New York: Norton, 1983.

Padilla, Elena. *Up from Puerto Rico*. New York: Columbia University Press, 1958.

Roberts, John Storm. *The Latin Tinge: The Impact of Latin American Music on the United States*. New York: Oxford University Press, 1979.

Rodríguez, Clara E. *Puerto Ricans: Born in the U.S.A.* Boston: Unwin Hyman, 1989.

Rogler, Lloyd H., and Rosemary Santana Cooney. *Puerto Rican Families in New York City: Intergenerational Processes*. Maplewood, NJ: Waterfront Press, 1984.

Steiner, Stan. *The Island: The World of the Puerto Ricans*. New York: Harper & Row, 1974.

Wagenheim, Kal. *Puerto Rico: A Profile*. New York: Praeger, 1970.

Wakefield, Dan. *Island in the City: The World of Spanish Harlem*. Boston: Houghton Mifflin, 1959.

INDEX

Africa, 24, 25
Algarin, Miguel, 81
Amadeo, king of Spain, 25
American Socialist party, 44
Aspira, 63, 65
Ateneo de Puerto Rico, 79
Autonomous Charter, 29

Badillo, Herman, 81, 83
Bilingualism, 14–15, 75
   in education, 15, 63
Blanco, 25
Bodegas, 14
Boleros, 94
Bonilla, Frank, 65
Borinquén, 22
Boston, Massachusetts, 66, 68, 76
Botánicas, 77
Brooklyn, New York, 45
Brooklyn Navy Yard, 13, 44
Bush, George, 36

Caballeros de San Juan, 67
California, 66, 69
Campo, Pupi, 95
Cancel Miranda, Rafael, 36
Caparra, 23
Caribbean Sea, 19, 22, 41
Casiano, Manuel A., Jr., 81
Census Bureau, U.S., 14, 59
Cepeda, Orlando Manuel, 88
Charles IV, king of Spain, 27
Chicago, Illinois, 66, 67, 68, 95
City University of New York, 64,
   65, 83
Clemente, Roberto, 87–88
Colón, Jesús, 81
Columbus, Christopher, 22–23, 39
Compadrazgo, 73–74
Congress, U.S., 20, 34, 35, 81, 83
Connecticut, 36, 47, 66, 67
Constitution, U.S., 20
Constitution Day, 35
Coordinator of Spanish Catholic
   Action, 76

Corrada, Alvaro, 76
Cortes, 28
Cruz, Celia, 96
Cuba, 19, 29, 30, 44, 75, 93
Cubans, 15, 67, 68
Curbelo, José, 95

De color, 25
Detroit, Michigan, 67, 97
Díaz, Justino, 93
Dominican Republic, 43, 75, 93
Down These Mean Streets (Thomas),
   84
Drake, Sir Francis, 26

East Harlem, New York, 45, 65, 83,
   84, 93
El Diario-La Prensa, 15
Elective Governors Act, 35
El Grito de Lares, 29
El Morro, 26
El Postillón, 43
Emeterio Betances, Ramón, 43
England, 26, 27
Escobar, Sixto, 84–85

Federación Libre de Trabajadores
   (FLT), 44
Feliciano, José, 97–98
Ferdinand, king of Spain, 23
Fernandez, Joseph A., 65–66
Ferré, Luis A., 29
Ferré, Maurice, 81
Ferrer, José, 89
Florida, 19, 66, 67, 81
Foraker Act, 30, 31
France, 27

Garcia, Robert, 81
Golden Streets, The (Thomas), 84
Gonzales, Robert, 76
Gonzalo "Pachin" Marin,
   Francisco, 43
Great Depression, 41, 45
Great migration, 48

Grifo, 25
Guánica, 30, 35
Guerra, Marcelino, 95
Guzman, Pablo, 81

"Hell's Kitchen," New York, 45
Hernández Colón, Rafael, 36
Hispanic Organization of Latin
    Actors (HOLA), 92
House of Delegates, 31
House of Representatives, U.S., 21,
    36, 82, 83
Humacao, 91
Hunger Project, 92

Iglesias Pantín, Santiago, 44
Illinois, 66
Independence party, 35
Independentistas, 36–37
Indio, 25
Instituto de Puerto Rico, 79
Isabella, queen of Spain, 23

Jones Act, 32
José de Diego School, 15
Julia, Raul, 84, 92–93

La Fortaleza, 26
Lares, 29, 97
Latin American music, 93–97
League of Patriots, 30, 43
Long Island, New York, 47, 67
Lorain, Ohio, 69
Los Angeles, California, 69, 95
Los Macheteros, 36
Lugo, Nick, 81
Luis Muñoz Marín Boulevard, 83

Machismo, 59–60
Machito, 95
Machito's Afro-Cubans, 94
María de Hostos, Eugenio, 30, 43
Marín, Ramón, 82
Marqués, René, 83–84
Martí, Frank, 95
Massachusetts, 66

Mateo Sagasta, Práxedes, 29
Menudo, 95
Miami, Florida, 19, 66, 67, 81, 95,
    96
Michigan, 47
Miles, Nelson A., 29
Moreno, Rita, 90–92
Morenos, 72
Muñoz Marín, Luis, 35, 36, 44,
    72–73, 78, 82
Muñoz Rivera, Luis, 44, 82

Nationalist party, 34
Negro/negra, 25
New Jersey, 47, 66, 67
New Orleans, Louisiana, 66
New Progressive party, 35–36
New York City, 13, 14, 15, 17, 43,
    44–45, 47–48, 57, 59, 60, 62–66,
    67, 68, 71, 74, 75, 76, 78, 79, 84,
    89, 90, 91, 92, 95, 96, 97, 102
Novelas, 15

Office of the Commonwealth of
    Puerto Rico, 47, 67, 78
Operation Bootstrap, 35
O'Reilly, Alexander, 27
Orlando, Tony, 81
Ortiz, Carlos, 85
Ox Cart, The (Marqués), 83–84

Pantoja, Antonia, 65
Pennsylvania, 66
Philadelphia, Pennsylvania, 68, 95,
    96
Piñero, Jesús T., 35
Plenas, 93
Ponce, 34, 81, 85, 93
Ponce de León, Juan, 23
Popular Democratic party, 36, 82
Power, Ramón, 27, 28
Prinze, Freddie, 81
Puente, Tito, 94, 95, 96, 97
Puerto Rican Family Institute, 74
Puerto Rican Federal Relations Act,
    35

Puerto Rican Forum, 79
Puerto Rican Merchants
  Association, 79
Puerto Ricans
  assimilation into U.S. society,
    72–73
  discrimination against, 47, 71–72
  education in U.S., 15, 62–66, 69,
    102
  employment in U.S., 61–62, 69
  family structure, 57, 58–60,
    73–74
  income level in U.S., 16, 48, 60,
    69
  as migrant farm workers, 45–47,
    78
  migration to U.S., 13–14, 22, 39,
    40, 41, 44–45, 47–48, 57, 58, 66,
    68, 101
  population in the U.S., 14, 15, 16
  poverty, 16, 57
  relations with black Americans,
    72
  and religion, 59, 69, 74–78
  as U.S. citizens, 13, 21, 32, 48,
    101
  in U.S. politics, 66, 69, 83
Puerto Ricans: Born in the U.S.A.
  (Rodríguez), 71
Puerto Rican Studies Center, 65
Puerto Rican studies programs, 65
Puerto Rican Teachers Association,
  79
Puerto Rico
  agricultural economy, 26, 34
  appeals for reform, 27–29
  class distinctions, 25
  climate, 19–20
  economy, 21, 26, 27, 30, 33, 35,
    41
  ethnic composition of, 25
  geography, 19
  independence movement, 21, 29,
    35–37, 43–44
  political status, 21, 35–37
  standard of living, 39

trade, 26, 27
  as a U.S. commonwealth, 20, 21,
    35, 37
  U.S. invasion, 30
  as a U.S. territory, 30–31
  vegetation and forestry, 20
  wildlife, 20

Quero Chiesa, Luis, 65, 79
Quiñones, José María, 28
Quiñones, Nathan, 65

Rivera, Chita, 89–90
Rivera, Geraldo, 81
Rodriguez, Juan A. "Chi Chi,"
  85–86
Rodriguez, Pablo "Tito," 94
Roosevelt, Theodore, Jr., 34
Roque, Julio, 93

Salsa, 15, 93
San Cristóbal, 26
San Francisco, California, 69
San Juan, 14, 23, 25, 26, 27, 47, 48,
  82, 85, 88, 92, 93, 94
Santana, Carlos, 97
Santiago Iglesias Day, 44
Santo Domingo, 43
Slavery, 24, 25, 26, 43
Smallpox, 24
Socialist party, 44
Spain, 19, 22, 23, 25, 26–30, 82
Spanish-American War, 19, 29–30
Spanish Harlem, 14, 44, 84, 95
Supreme Court, U.S., 35

Taino Indians, 22–24, 25
Thomas, Piri, 81, 84
Treaty of Paris, 30
Trigueno, 25, 71
Truman, Harry S., 36

United States Catholic Conference,
  76
Universidad Boricua (Puerto Rican
  University), 65

Valdez, Miguelito, 95
Valens, Ritchie, 95

Washington, D.C., 65, 76, 82, 90
West Side Story, 45, 90, 91, 92
White, Vanna, 81
Wilson, Woodrow, 32

World War I, 13, 44
World War II, 13, 41, 45, 47, 48, 66, 67, 69, 78, 95

Young Lords, 65
Youngstown, Ohio, 69

JEROME J. ALIOTTA is a freelance writer and editor and has taught in New York City public high schools. Born in Detroit, Michigan, he holds a bachelor's degree from the University of Michigan and a master's degree from New York University, both in English literature. He lives in New York City and is working on a collection of short stories.

SANDRA STOTSKY is director of the Institute on Writing, Reading, and Civic Education at the Harvard Graduate School of Education as well as a research associate there. She is also editor of *Research in the Teaching of English,* a journal sponsored by the National Council of Teachers of English.

Dr. Stotsky holds a bachelor of arts degree with distinction from the University of Michigan and a doctorate in education from the Harvard Graduate School of Education. She has taught on the elementary and high school levels and at Northeastern University, Curry College, and Harvard. Her work in education has ranged from serving on academic advisory boards to developing elementary and secondary curricula as a consultant to the Polish Ministry of Education. She has written numerous scholarly articles, curricular materials, encyclopedia entries, and reviews and is the author or co-author of three books on education.

REBECCA STEFOFF is a writer and editor who has published more than 50 nonfiction books for young adults. Many of her books deal with geography, environmental issues, and exploration, including the three-volume set *Extraordinary Explorers.* She has worked with Ronald Takaki in adapting *Strangers from a Distant Shore* into a 15-volume Chelsea House series, the ASIAN AMERICAN EXPERIENCE. Stefoff studied English at the University of Pennsylvania, where she taught for three years. She lives in Portland, Oregon.

REED UEDA is associate professor of history at Tufts University. He graduated summa cum laude with a bachelor of arts degree from UCLA, received master of arts degrees from both the University of Chicago and Harvard University, and received a doctorate in history from Harvard.

Dr. Ueda was research editor of the *Harvard Encyclopedia of American Ethnic Groups* and has served on the board of editors for *American Quarterly, Harvard Educational Review, Journal of Interdisciplinary History,* and *University of Chicago School Review.* He is the author of several books on ethnic studies, including *Postwar Immigrant America: A Social History, Ethnic Groups in History Textbooks,* and *Immigration.*

DANIEL PATRICK MOYNIHAN is the senior United States senator from New York. He is also the only person in American history to serve in the cabinets or subcabinets of four successive presidents–Kennedy, Johnson, Nixon, and Ford. Formerly a professor of government at Harvard University, he has written and edited many books, including *Beyond the Melting Pot, Ethnicity: Theory and Experience* (both with Nathan Glazer), *Loyalties*, and *Family and Nation.*

Picture Credits